D. H. Lawrence and the New World

D. H. Lawrence
and the New World

DAVID CAVITCH

New York
OXFORD UNIVERSITY PRESS
1969

For Joan and Max

Acknowledgments

I am grateful to many scholars and colleagues who read portions of this study at various stages of its completion, and I wish to acknowledge especially the aid of Frederick C. Crews. His comments and questions repeatedly helped me to gain better understanding of my subject. Throughout my work I have benefited from Mark Schorer's generative essays on Lawrence, recently reprinted in *The World We Imagine*.

I am grateful also to the American Philosophical Society for a grant-in-aid that supported my writing during the summer of 1967.

The eighth chapter of this study was previously published in different form in *The Massachusetts Review*.

Permission to use quotations from works protected by copyright has been granted by:

The Viking Press, Inc., for quotations from *The Letters of D. H. Lawrence*, edited by Aldous Huxley (Copyright 1932 by the Estate of D. H. Lawrence, copyright © renewed 1960 by Angelo Ravagli and C. Montague Weekley, Executors of The Estate of Frieda Lawrence Ravagli); for quotations from *The Collected Letters of D. H. Lawrence*, edited by Harry T.

Moore (Copyright © 1962 by Angelo Ravagli and C. Montague Weekley, Executors of the Estate of Frieda Lawrence Ravagli, 1932 by The Estate of D. H. Lawrence and 1934 by Frieda Lawrence, © 1933, 1948, 1953, 1954 and each year 1956–1962 by Angelo Ravagli and C. Montague Weekley, Executors of the Estate of Frieda Lawrence Ravagli); for quotations from *Phoenix II: Uncollected, Unpublished, and Other Prose Works by D. H. Lawrence*, edited by Warren Roberts and Harry T. Moore (Copyright 1925 by Alfred A. Knopf, Inc., renewed 1953 by Frieda Lawrence Ravagli, Copyright © 1963 by the Estate of Frieda Lawrence Ravagli); for quotations from *The Rainbow* by D. H. Lawrence (Copyright 1915 by David Herbert Lawrence, renewed 1943 by Frieda Lawrence); for quotations from *Sea and Sardinia* by D. H. Lawrence (Copyright 1931 by Thomas Seltzer, Inc., renewed 1949 by Frieda Lawrence); for quotations from *Aaron's Rod* by D. H. Lawrence (Copyright 1922 by Thomas Seltzer, Inc., renewed 1950 by Frieda Lawrence); for quotations from *Apocalypse* by D. H. Lawrence (Copyright 1931 by The Estate of David Herbert Lawrence); for quotations from *The Complete Poems of D. H. Lawrence*, Volume I, edited by Vivian de Sola Pinto and F. Warren Roberts (Copyright 1923, renewed 1951 by Frieda Lawrence); for quotations from *The Complete Poems of D. H. Lawrence*, Volume II, edited by Vivian de Sola Pinto and F. Warren Roberts (Copyright 1933 by Frieda Lawrence); for quotations from *Etruscan Places* by D. H. Lawrence (Originally published by The Viking Press, Inc., in 1932); for quotations from *Kangaroo* by D. H. Lawrence (Copyright 1923 by Thomas Seltzer, Inc., renewed 1951 by Frieda Lawrence); for quotations from *Phoenix: The Posthumous Papers of D. H. Lawrence*, edited by Edward D. McDonald (Copyright 1936 by Frieda Lawrence, copyright © renewed 1964 by the Estate of the late Frieda Lawrence Ravagli); for quotations from *Sons and Lovers* by D. H. Lawrence (Copyright 1913 by Thomas Seltzer, Inc.); for quotations from *Studies in Classic American Literature*, by D. H. Lawrence (Copyright 1923, renewed 1951 by Frieda Lawrence); for quotations from *The Complete Short Stories of D. H. Lawrence*, Volume I; for quotations from *Women in Love*, by D. H. Lawrence (Copyright 1920, 1922 by David Herbert Lawrence, renewed 1948, 1950 by Frieda Lawrence); for quotations from *The Symbolic Meaning: the Uncollected Versions of "Studies in Classic American Literature,"* edited by Armin Arnold (Copyright 1923, renewed 1951 by Frieda Lawrence, Copyright © 1961 by the Estate of the late Mrs. Frieda Lawrence).

Harcourt, Brace & World, Inc., for quotations from *The Letters of Ezra Pound, 1907–1941.*

William Heinemann Limited and Laurence Pollinger Limited, for quotations from "The Princess," and *Lady Chatterley's Lover*, by D. H. Lawrence (from the Estate of the late Mrs. Frieda Lawrence).

Alfred A. Knopf, Inc., for quotations from *Mornings in Mexico*, by D. H. Lawrence (Copyright 1927 by Alfred A. Knopf, Inc., renewed 1955 by Frieda Lawrence Ravagli); for quotations from *The Plumed Serpent*, by D. H. Lawrence (Copyright 1926 by Alfred A. Knopf, Inc., renewed 1954 by Frieda Lawrence Ravagli); for quotations from "The Woman Who Rode Away," by D. H. Lawrence (Copyright 1927 by Alfred A. Knopf, Inc., renewed 1955 by Frieda Lawrence Ravagli); for quotations from "St. Mawr" and "The Man Who Died," in *The Later D. H. Lawrence*, edited by William York Tindall, 1952.

There is no authoritative text for any of Lawrence's novels, and as several inexpensive editions are easily available all references to the novels are cited by chapter numbers alone. Standard editions of collected writings are cited by page number and the following abbreviations:

CL *The Collected Letters of D. H. Lawrence*, edited by Harry T. Moore, Viking Press, 1962.

CP *The Complete Poems of D. H. Lawrence*, edited by Vivian De Sola Pinto and Warren Roberts, Viking Press, 1964.

LH *The Letters of D. H. Lawrence*, edited by Aldous Huxley, Viking Press, 1932.

P *Phoenix: The Posthumous Papers of D. H. Lawrence*, edited by Edward McDonald, Viking Press, 1936.

P2 *Phoenix Two: Uncollected, Unpublished, and Other Prose Works by D. H. Lawrence*, edited by Warren Roberts and Harry T. Moore, Viking Press, 1968.

T *The Tales of D. H. Lawrence*, Secker, 1934.

Contents

"The whole of life is one long, blind effort at an established polarity with the outer universe, human and non-human; and the whole of modern life is a shrieking failure. It is our own fault."

Psychoanalysis and the Unconscious

D. H. Lawrence and the New World

1

"Art for my sake"

For D. H. Lawrence writing was part of a unified effort to expand and perfect the entire arena of human experience. He allied his art with polemical attempts to engage other people in constructing, or at least considering, some form of comprehensive order that would make the world less difficult to live in. For many of his adult years he hoped to lead a vanguard of personal followers into a new world of psychically liberated, sensual experience by guiding them into accepting their non-rational selves and trusting the fundamental good nature of one another. He brought that effort and other themes of his life into his writing to make them subjects of direct analysis and experimentation; always recognizably autobiographical or self-dramatizing, his art directs our attention to his beliefs and his pursuit of "ultimate marriage," or a utopian retreat, or a theocratic state, or to his constant search for relationships in which spontaneous passions flow easily among people. He brings the reader forcibly into his works as well, for his characteristic mode of writing invites the reader's heated participation in the author's dialectics. "Whoever reads me will be in the thick of the scrimmage," he warned, "and if he doesn't like it—if he wants a safe seat in the audience—let him read somebody else." (*CL* 827)

Lawrence believed that the key to greater self-realization is the body's natural wisdom of its immediate desires and aversions. The person who achieves a subtle awareness of his unconscious sympathies would fulfill his individual self through profound, active relations with other individuals, with nature and, possibly, with a reorganized society. "My great religion is a belief in the blood, the flesh, as being wiser than the intellect," he explained in an early letter that states his beliefs as a newly matured writer:

> We can go wrong in our minds. But what our blood feels and believes and says, is always true. The intellect is only a bit and a bridle. What do I care about knowledge. All I want is to answer to my blood, direct, without fribbling intervention of mind, or moral, or what-not. I conceive a man's body as a kind of flame, like a candle flame, forever upright and yet flowing: and the intellect is just the light that is shed on to the things around. And I am not so much concerned with the things around—which is really mind—but with the mystery of the flame forever flowing, coming God knows how from out of practically nowhere, and being *itself*, whatever there is around it, that it lights up. We have got so ridiculously mindful, that we never know that we ourselves are anything—we think there are only the objects we shine upon. And there the poor flame goes on burning ignored, to produce this light. And instead of chasing the mystery in the fugitive, half-lighted things outside us, we ought to look at ourselves, and say "My God, I am myself!" That is why I like to live in Italy. The people are so unconscious. They only feel and want: they don't know. We know too much. No, we only *think* we know such a lot. A flame isn't a flame because it lights up two, or twenty objects on a

table. It's a flame because it is itself. And we have forgotten ourselves. We are Hamlet without the Prince of
Denmark. We cannot *be*. "To be or not to be"—it is the
question with us now, by Jove. And nearly every Englishman says "Not to be." So he goes in for Humani-
tarianism and such-like forms of not-being. The real
way of living is to answer to one's wants. Not "I want to
light up with my intelligence as many things as possible"
but "For the living of my full flame—I want that
liberty, I want that woman, I want that pound of
peaches, I want to go to sleep, I want to go to the pub
and have a good time, I want to look a beastly swell
today, I want to kiss that girl, I want to insult that
man." Instead of that, all these wants, which are there
whether-or-not, are utterly ignored, and we talk about
some sort of ideas. I'm like Carlyle, who, they say,
wrote 50 volumes on the value of silence. (*CL* 180)

Lawrence at times despaired of humanity, because he saw
modern man as mortally afraid of spontaneous feelings. The
state of contemporary civilization was evidence to him that
man now repudiates his bodily life. Society's ideals, which are
the rationalizations of our self-denial and self-hate, substitute
controlled, conceptual experience—"Subdue the flesh,"
"Love your neighbor"—for the concreteness and variety of a
person's sensual responses. Man becomes increasingly a product of his unbalanced civilization—a social rather than a natural creature, perpetuating the maladies of his society—and his
natural manhood withers along with his diminishing capacity
and freedom to be himself, openly.

Lawrence's writing was guided always by his desire to
break down the barriers to spontaneity and to reintegrate our
submerged, fundamental selves with our overt lives. The
integration and destiny of essential human identity, across
centuries or generations or within single life-spans or in brief

moments of vitalization, interested him more than the circumstantial and conscious developments in the lives of his characters. His art, however fully it represents objective details of
historical and personal life, focuses chiefly upon the recesses of
individual consciousness, where his characters encounter their
generic, natural self and must make a crucial adjustment to it.
In writing to remind people of their fundamental identity—
"we never know that we ourselves are anything"—Lawrence's stance is sometimes prophetic and visionary with
apocalyptic utterances, but he is almost always hortatory to
some degree, as even his letters illustrate. He felt that art
could serve man's urgent need to reclaim his essential being.
The integration of character which Lawrence understood as
necessary could come about through freeing our emotions
from the tangle and oppression of our rational thought. Apart
from the possibly restorative powers of passional experience,
as in sexual intercourse or deeply felt encounters with death,
only the strong feelings of an aesthetic response can renew
man's awareness of his sensual identity and direct him toward
acceptance of his whole self. Literature and painting, the arts
which Lawrence practiced and wrote about, have a corrective
moral effect; by reviving the individual's capacity for direct,
pre-mental responses, great art works can tear a hole in the
curtain of mental consciousness and alter the way men recognize their lives thereafter. No protagonist in Lawrence's fiction has his sensuality revivified by reading a good book or at-
tending an exhibition, but Lawrence assumed that his readers
might profit from opportunities that his characters go without. The novel particularly, Lawrence came to feel, "can in-
form and lead into new places the flow of our sympathetic
consciousness, and it can lead our sympathy away in recoil
from things gone dead."

But the artist himself, Lawrence was aware, is also affected by the ideology of his era, and his conscious mind also tends to suppress the life of his body; so that the artist even while working creatively is in danger of succumbing to the falsifications of a social ethos or of his own repressive character. He must constantly struggle against his tendencies to blur his awareness of subjective reality or to distort his account of it, and he must learn not to interfere with his intuition of experience. "I think one has as it were to fuse one's physical and mental self right down, to produce good art." (*CL* 251) Insofar as the artist can achieve the honest expression of his whole emotion, he has for the time integrated his physical and his mental halves. Art can be restorative at very least for the artist.

Lawrence felt that his art was personally therapeutic, that is, only his creative work enabled him to live sanely and in close contact with the reality of his experience. His writing was intentionally an exploration of his own soul. In a Foreword to *Women in Love*, a novel which makes emphatic assertions about civilizations and mankind generally, Lawrence wrote: "This novel pretends only to be a record of the writer's own desires, aspirations, struggles; in a word, a record of the profoundest experiences in the self." Recognizing that like all men he was a partial victim of his own troubled consciousness, he wrote to examine the truth of *his* nature, whatever generalizations he extrapolated with reference to humanity or the present state of civilization. Writing, he believed, was part of "the passionate struggle into conscious being," and it could untie the knots that bound him to repeat old feelings. In *Sons and Lovers* he recapitulated much of his actual past in an effort to understand his continuing emotions about it and to liberate himself for a freer response to the present.

"One sheds one's sicknesses in books," he said soon after finishing the novel—"repeats and presents again one's emotions, to be master of them." (*CL* 234) He described his satisfaction from even his casual watercolors as immediately "healing," "soothing," "refreshing," and his justifications of creative activity in general point neither to the art object nor to its reference in the actual world but to the psychological needs of the artist. "I always say, my motto is 'Art for my sake,'" he remarked in a gay formulation of his most serious aesthetic. (*LH* 88)

The emotional coherence of a work was his principal standard of evaluation, and he saw the art of writing as a continuous experiment with the formal possibilities of uncovering new emotional substance. To open up new feelings, he required newly expressive forms. He expected each emotion to take an original shape that might at times result in an innovative, unconventional work; and he condemned the practiced skill of the writer who repeats the forms of his tradition, concentrating principally on arranging the elements of his story or poem. As he saw his own task, "the difficulty is to find exactly the form one's passion . . . wants to take." (*LH* 88) What receives supreme value in Lawrence's aesthetic is that the form of a work should correspond to the emotional pattern in the consciousness of the artist. "I have always tried to get an emotion out in its own course, without altering it," Lawrence explained to a critic who thought that his verse lacked polish. "It needs the finest instinct imaginable, much finer than the skill of the craftsman." (*CL* 221) When Edward Marsh continued to point out metrical irregularities in his lines, Lawrence wrote again to maintain that "it is the hidden *emotional* pattern that makes poetry, not the obvious form." (*CL* 243)

In these early statements about his poetry, Lawrence's views coincide with the more fully articulated theories of Ezra Pound and other innovators before the first World War, who also were seeking to extend poetry's range of possible feelings by introducing freer rhythms. Pound had already stated in the *Poetry Review* that any good poem is governed not by conventional metrical patterns but by an " 'Absolute Rhythm,' a rhythm, that is, in poetry which corresponds exactly to an emotion or shade of emotion to be expressed. A man's rhythm must be interpretative, it will be, therefore, in the end, his own, uncounterfeiting, uncounterfeitable." [1] In apprising Harriet Monroe of current English poetry, Pound cited Lawrence for his innovative manner: "I think he learned the proper treatment of modern subjects before I did." [2] Months later, in a review of Lawrence's first volume of poems, Pound praised him for raising poetry up to modern standards of achievement.[3] But Lawrence's anti-traditionalism actually led him away from the goals of his immediate contemporaries, for the modernist movement in poetry and criticism devised a succession of formulas and catchwords for the common purpose of diverting attention from the artist's sensibility: Imagism, the objective correlative, the mask, Objectivism, or the pronouncement that art is "an escape from personality." The chief tenet of modernism, stated by Pound as "direct treatment of the thing, whether objective or subjective," could only mean for Lawrence that the whole treatment of a thing would include the reflection of the artist who was at every moment interpreting it. The main stream of modernist theory during Lawrence's life flowed toward the depersonalization of art, while Lawrence grew more consistent in his view that the sensibility of the artist should appear unhindered and undisguised in his work.

Lawrence argued that the writer should not attempt to efface himself, for deliberate anonymity in writing draws attention only to the author's pretense of impartiality. A writer should speak without self-consciousness in his own voice, which is the most honest articulation of his feelings. In the Foreword to *Women in Love* Lawrence defends his characteristically repetitive and incantatory phrasing by admitting that "the only answer is that it is natural to the author." He felt that his work gained authority by reflecting his temperament and idiosyncracies, because the acknowledged presence of the speaker underscored the aptness and the limitations of his utterance in relation to the times and the bias of its composition. "Away with eternal truth," he declared when he came to criticize the hidden bias of the classic American authors. "Truth lives from day to day, and the marvellous Plato of yesterday is chiefly bosh today." Art, he might have generalized, does not "imitate" or "mirror" the details of an objective or an eternal reality, except as it reveals primarily the truth of a man's emotional life in his time. He considered the elements of style mainly as they reflect the consciousness of the author; he regarded form as the expression of a unique emotion; and he spoke of a work's *viewpoint* as the bias that comes necessarily from the author's feeling. Unequivocally Romantic in his critical conceptions, he valued Art, including his own, for its expression of the artist's sensibility.

Lawrence's expressionism remains partially discredited even to this day by criticism that echoes R. P. Blackmur's statement that Lawrence's intensely personal art is mainly "hysteria." Lawrence was wrong, Blackmur argues, in believing "that if a thing is only intensely enough felt its mere expression in words will give it satisfactory form." [4] But Lawrence explained on several occasions that an emotion which is sensitively rendered in its wholeness articulates its own limits and creates an adequately complex form without requiring supervision from conventional, external guidelines.[5] Any emotion, Lawrence recognized, takes its character from the dynamics of the whole human situation in which it is experienced, which includes its resistant or counter feeling that is part of the state in which feeling occurs and gains force. The whole truth of any emotion includes an awareness of the conflict or complexities that limit it, and those limitations will appear in the formal qualities of the art, presumably as tension, paradox, irony, rational structure—all the shibboleths of the new criticism. Until very late in his life, Lawrence believed that order was a natural property of man's unconsciousness and that art restored the natural principle and made that order manifest. But the undisciplined outpouring of emotive language was to him the product of a blunting or disfiguring consciousness. When an acquaintance wrote her memoirs in what seemed to be truly a state of hysteria, Lawrence instructed her: "It's not art, because art always gilds the pill, and this is hemlock in a cup." (*CL* 900)

Lawrence thought that faulty art occurs when the artist's consciousness shuts out sensual knowledge and denies the full experiential world. His mind asserts itself as a cohesive, infinite universe, abrogating or identifying with the world outside it, and abstracting all phenomena into intellectual operations that can delude the ego. Lawrence's most important failure, *The Plumed Serpent*, illustrates his theory of how art fails, for the novel is impelled largely by his own futile effort to falsify sexual fears that he could no longer bear to acknowledge. The bad art that issues from facile or desperate self-deception is usually described by Lawrence as *sensationalism, egotism* or *ecstasy*, his key terms of critical disapproval.

"For God's sake," he answered one correspondent, "mistrust and beware of these states of exaltation and ecstasy. . . . There is no real truth in ecstasy. All vital truth contains the memory of that for which it is not true. Ecstasy achieves itself by virtue of exclusion; and in making any passionate exclusion, one has already put one's right hand in the hand of the lie." (*CL* 300)

Because any artist is implicated in the general distortions and limitations of consciousness, he must devise methods of expression which surpass his conscious understanding and rational viewpoint even while giving voice to them. The complexities of life that are often too intractable for coherent personal vision cannot be excluded from the art work, or the art produced will be mere self-advertisement: sensational, egotistic, ecstatic. To circumvent the limitations of personal, rational cognition and to make art effectively analytic, exploratory and revelatory for artist and audience alike, Lawrence trusted the power of his intuition to represent reality as it is. He equated intuition with direct "sensual knowledge," and he valued intuitive cognitions as more complex than rational ideas and impressions. "By intuition alone," he stated, "can man *really* be aware of man, or of the living, substantial world." In reflecting on the difficulty of communicating one's profound intuitions, Lawrence came to see that all good art is a symbolic language. Symbolism expresses what the mind cannot accurately formulate, or perhaps even accept, in discursive, rational terms. "I think there is the dual way of looking at things," Lawrence explained to the writer whom he cautioned against ecstasy. There is "our way, which is to say 'I am all. All other things are but radiation out from me.'— The other way is to try to conceive the whole, to build up a whole by means of symbolism, because symbolism avoids the

I and puts aside the egotist; and in the whole, to take our decent place." (*CL* 302)

But since the symbol assumes its form within the limitations of person and circumstance that call for its use, those same limitations need to be identified. In Lawrence's work generally, his authorial presence in self-portraits or in the signatory marks of his unusual sensibility maintains an internal relationship between the living artist and the symbolic universe of his poem or fiction. The visible Lawrence appears in the subject material of his art as a formal element arising from his insistence that art should refer to the particular human condition from which it is created. He gives himself away, and the result of the disclosure is to distinguish his personal motives and passions from his insight which is the larger symbolic meaning of each work as a whole.

The formal complexity of Lawrence's art goes unnoticed by the reader who registers only the passion of advocacy by which he tested a variety of viewpoints. He tested his beliefs, his life, and his readers with an insistent pressure to discover and destroy all that is counterfeit and distorted in our conceptions of reality. He strained his own conscious understanding to the task of proving his intuitions, and because of the urgency of his manner one can easily fail to recognize the qualifying effects of Lawrence's methods and tones. He never neglected to point out his own person involved in the fray of thinking and feeling, and his self-disclosures acknowledge the private and limited authority behind his judgments. In the midst of passionate efforts to realize a new and freer world, part of him undertook to keep a critical eye on Lawrence.

2

"A woman at the back of me"

Lawrence was twenty-seven when he finished writing *Sons and Lovers*. He was living in a lakeside village in northern Italy where he recently had come with Frieda, who was five years his senior, the mother of three children and the wife of his former French professor. The lovers had eloped from Nottingham after a six weeks' acquaintance and had traveled to Germany where Frieda's explanations to her family and her uncertainties about returning to England kept Lawrence waiting restively in the Rhineland. Then, in an idyll of initial privacy in love, Lawrence and Frieda walked and sojourned down the Isar valley and crossed through the Tyrol, journeying toward Lake Garda in Italy. When they arrived and had fairly well established their ménage of bohemian exile, Lawrence wrote to his editor in September 1912, "I am glad to be settling down, to get at that novel. I am rather keen on it." (*CL* 143)

Sons and Lovers, the largely autobiographical story of Paul Morel, is the first piece of fiction that Lawrence completed in the new circumstances of his life with Frieda, and their relationship was the largest single aid in Lawrence's astonishing development from the level of apprenticeship in his earlier two novels to the artfulness of his third book.[1] When his mother died in 1911, Lawrence had emerged from youth with little confidence or stamina remaining for further life. For months he was ill with pneumonia, and his inner "demon," as he sometimes called his creative self, nearly died of attrition, unable to grow beyond a youthful, winsomely sad awareness of delicate beauty—an effete response to life that is characteristic of Lawrence's early works. The liaison with Frieda was a total revitalization, and he later regarded the period of his romance as a rebirth of creative and moral energy after an experience of despair:

> In that year [1911], for me everything collapsed, save the mystery of death, and the haunting of death in life. I was twenty-five, and from the death of my mother, the world began to dissolve around me, beautiful, iridescent, but passing away substanceless. Till I almost dissolved away myself, and was very ill: when I was twenty-six.
> Then slowly the world came back: or I myself returned: but to another world. And in 1912, when I was still twenty-six, the other phase commenced, the phase of *Look! We Have Come Through!*—when I left teaching, and left England, and left many other things, and the demon had a new run for his money. (P 253)

Lawrence's return "to another world," the phase that is celebrated in the cycle of love-poems that he mentions, coincided with his new love for Frieda, who was an example to him and perhaps even an apostle of faith in the spontaneous, passionate self. At their first meetings he was dazzled by her emotional freedom, describing her as "perfectly unconventional, but really good"; and when he soon met her sisters he was amazed to find similar qualities in them: they were proudly sensual and morally emancipated women. "Lord, what a family. I've never seen anything like it," he wrote from Germany. (*CL* 115) What he saw so strikingly in Frieda's life-style was a degree of autonomy that he urgently needed in his own life, and with her companionship he began to achieve it. In their illicit love and their elopement and eventual marriage they largely transcended conventional morality and disregarded the standards of their social classes. Their more or less necessary exile averted Lawrence's return to the dreaded task of provincial schoolteaching. He spoke of having freed himself from "England" as a sign that with Frieda he could also overcome the psychological barriers to a fuller life and a unified identity. From Germany he wrote: "I loathe the idea of England, and its enervation and misty miserable modernness. I don't want to go back to town and civilization. I want to rough it and scramble through free, free. I *don't* want to be tied down. And I can live on a tiny bit. I shan't let F. leave me, if I can help it. I feel I've got a mate and I'll fight tooth and claw to keep her. She says I'm reverting, but I'm not—I'm only coming out wholesome and myself. . . . I *loathe Paul Morel.*" (*CL* 135)

If it is true, as some biographers allege, that by marrying Frieda, Lawrence shifted the burden of his emotional dependency from his mother to his wife,[2] it is nevertheless most clear that even the limited triumph directly served his genius for art and for living. He gained a sense of freedom that may have been in excess of his actual circumstances, but it still helped him for the remaining eighteen years of his life to gain ground against fatalism. Direct comparison of the two women, however, suggests the more likely possibility that Frieda was the surprising embodiment of everything that Lawrence had wished his mother to be, so that he might love her without being trapped by her neurotic demands on his emotions. Frieda was a buoyantly independent, sensual, proud, intellectual, and expansive woman. That Lydia Lawrence was nothing of the sort[3] had always roused her loving son's anxieties and guilt. His sense of complicity in her failure as a person was a cause of continuing distress, as *Sons and Lovers* reveals by his attempts to disguise her actual shortcomings beyond what the fiction requires or his own artistic honesty can permit. His conscious characterization of Gertrude Morel represents his ideal for his mother more closely than it portrays Lydia Lawrence, and it was impossible for Lawrence until years later to acknowledge any considerable unattractiveness in his mother's character. Frieda, however, was the ideal woman who proved to be real, and his response to her was not a simple neurotic transference but a fairly free emotional commitment to a person whose love offered him partial liberation from both psychic and circumstantial bondage.

His joyful sense of escape from the limitations of his former life gave him the will and the opportunity to win a similar freedom for his inward-turning imagination. From the actual changes in his life Lawrence acquired a broader perspective of experience and a more analytical intelligence to consider that side of his nature which was Paul Morel. Frieda actively participated in his work as he went about revising the earlier manuscript. He read parts of his fresh writing to her and questioned her about the soundness of the characterizations. Frieda's own letters to Edward Garnett, Lawrence's editor, defend the novel's "honesty" and "vividness" against Garnett's insistence upon matters of "form." "Any new thing must find a new shape," she says, echoing Lawrence's own attitude. It is unlikely, though, that she merely echoed Lawrence when together they examined particular details of the fiction. "He is writing P.M. again," she reported to Garnett, "reads bits to me and we fight like blazes over it, he is so often beside the point, 'but "I'll learn him to be a toad" as the boy said as he stamped on the toad.'" Frieda says that she "wrote little female bits and lived it over in my own heart." [4] She recalled that "when he wrote his mother's death he was ill and his grief made me ill too." [5] As Lawrence re-created the stresses of his family relations and again suffered through some of the worst episodes of his past, her empathy gave him another avenue to the truth of experience. With generous egotism he began advising other young writers and artists to rely more on the sensitivity and power of women. He felt that the works of his contemporaries were flawed by ignoring or falsifying the feminine reality. Garnett was writing a play about Joan of Arc: "You've got a fair amount of 'priest' in you," Lawrence stated after reading the manuscript. "It's the *positivity* of women you seem to deny—make them sort of instrumental. There is in women such a big sufficiency unto themselves, more than in men." (*CL* 157) He cautioned an illustrator who wrote him after submitting dust-jacket designs for *Sons and Lovers*:

> You are more or less a Galahad—which is not, I believe, good for your art. It is hopeless for me to do anything without I have a woman at the back of me. And you seem a bit like that—not hopeless—but too uncertain. Böcklin—or somebody like him—daren't sit in a cafe except with his back to the wall. I daren't sit in the world without a woman behind me. And you give me that feeling a bit: as if you were uneasy of what is behind you. Excuse me if I am wrong. But a woman that I love sort of keeps me in direct communication with the unknown, in which otherwise I am a bit lost. (*CL* 179)

The marital relation was essential not only to sustain Lawrence's ability to work, but also because woman was his major contact with unforeknown experience, his "communication with the unknown." He implies in his letter that he can discern the unconscious and mysterious operations of life more clearly in woman's sensibility than in man's, and this affinity for the private feminine response is characteristic of many of Lawrence's best works. Frieda could not have had such an extraordinary, salutary effect on Lawrence's creativity had not his genius needed to identify and empathize with womankind.

Even in his first two books Lawrence attends principally to the female reality, to the degree that some reviewers thought that the unfamiliar author was a woman. The peculiar focus of those novels is relevant to part of his achievement in *Sons and Lovers*. In *The White Peacock* (1911) Lawrence creates the fully engaging girl Lettie, whose calculating choice of Leslie as a socially valuable husband destroys her own integrity and breaks the spirit of her more sensual lover, George. The story of this triangle of youthful friends is narrated by Cyril, Lettie's brother, who is diffidently involved with Emily, who is George's sister. George's catastrophic marriage to slatternly Meg and his consequent physical and emotional degeneration illustrate the dangers of sexual life that further inhibit Cyril's responsiveness to women, and his aborted romance with Emily fades from the narrative as she marries outside of her neighborhood group. Lettie, ever beautiful and proud, assumes her station in life that is symbolized by the pale, vain bird that defiles the roost.

Each of the young men in the novel yields to his disappointing fate without much fight against it, and all three are overwhelmed and overshadowed by the demands, the resistances, and the vividness of the women, who clearly show more force and freedom to guide their own lives even though they pathetically abide by the values of refinement or maternal domesticity. Yet there is only a very feeble sensuality which the men in this book can offer as an alternative to gentility; each of them is fragile, and the sensual nature of George and even of the older gamekeeper, Annable, leads both men into bitter, degenerate animality that is their destruction. Cyril, at his best, is "the sad, departing observer of the breakup of a cherished, but irretrievably disintegrated way of life," as one critic has described him; and Cyril's priggishness and nostalgia sentimentalize the entire drama about young sexuality.[6] As an observer he contributes no insight to what, exactly, has been lost from life; and his limited view of events does not include even circumstantial causes—the *how* and *when* explanations —of the deep sense of loss in all these exquisite young lives.[7] Through Cyril's filmy *Weltschmerz* only Lettie's powerful but misdirected self-assertiveness strikes a spark of convincing vitality for the reader.

Lawrence's characterizations of women are more successful and more prominent than those of the men in his next novel also. *The Trespasser* (1912) is the story of Helena's tragic affair with Siegmund who commits suicide when his relations with his repugnant wife and with his adored mistress prove to be almost equally unfulfilling. The account of the lovers' crucial holiday together and its catastrophic aftermath is told as a flashback. Helena's subsequent friendship with Cecil Byrne frames the central narrative, and the method of narration gives Cecil the foreground position of a compassionate, forbearing observer who would like to recompense Helena with his own love. Cecil, like Cyril, is an affected, epicene, vague young man whose soft, transparent heart is his only credit. Siegmund's small amount of courage for life is depleted by the difficult effort to begin, in tired middle-age, a strenuous love affair with a younger woman whose maternal response in love

he ambivalently clamors for and deplores. But his extreme reactions and his half-created character are never clearly seen
even by the novelist. Helena is the only fully actualized
figure, and her whole experience with Siegmund, which is
thrown into a niche of time by the method of narration, seems
not so real as Lawrence's representation of her complicated
sensibility. "Helena," says Richard Aldington in his Introduction to the Phoenix edition, "is almost the most interesting of
all Lawrence's women characters"; and Aldington's "almost-
the-most-of-all" stumble toward expression speaks for Helena's substantiality in a novel that does not support her with
an adequately convincing context, or world.

When Lawrence turned to writing *Sons and Lovers* a good
deal of Cyril and Cecil persisted into his characterization of
Paul, for Paul retains some of their vague transparency
through which we view more substantial figures, especially
Mrs. Morel. Certainly Lawrence's new life with Frieda intensified his literary interest in the female character, and this
book which Lawrence supposed was very closely autobiographical is dominated by the figure not of Paul, but of Paul's
mother. "The mother is really the thread, the domineering
note," Frieda explained when in her letter to Garnett she de-
fended the form of the novel. The narrative events, rear-
ranged in chronological order, begin with Mrs. Morel's romantic girlhood and conclude immediately after her death,
which is the event of deepest pathos and most complex
presentation in the fiction. Though the story is securely Paul's
—that is, we are interested in what happens to *him*, and our
suspense is engaged by what will happen next to him—
Gertrude Morel governs the plot of the novel. She promotes
William's and Paul's ambitions that distinguish them from
other workingmen's children in Eastwood; and her power of

will is the chief human control over the actions of all her family and over the fates of those who come into contact with it, like young William's and Paul's unlucky mistresses. Paul's story is his struggle to transcend the ambivalent love linking him to his mother, a passion which he partially evaluates in his affairs with Miriam and Clara, for the girls mirror aspects of the infinite variety that Mrs. Morel has in the eyes of her son. But in Paul's problematic growth toward manhood Gertrude introduces more than the general human fate of Oedipal love from which he must win some measure of personal freedom. Gertrude Morel does not play the same passive role as Hamlet's Gertrude, who enters no rivalry with Ophelia. For all her other vagaries, the Queen never directly tampered with Hamlet's sexual development. In *Sons and Lovers*, however, Gertrude Morel's increasing attachment to Paul and her initiative in their romance make up a large part of the dramatic action, and to his terrible disadvantage Paul is an *ingenu*.

Gertrude's first lover is a weak-willed suitor who gives up his romance and his wish to become a minister when his father pushes him into a business career. When she later meets Walter Morel, his workingman's aplomb and warm-hearted sensuality reassure her that being a *man* is indeed "everything"—the ideal that her former lover had ignobly denied. For months after their marriage, Gertrude is thoroughly happy with Walter, but when she discovers how much of his cheer masks an attitude of irresponsibility for his family and even for his own pride and manhood, her love turns to hostility which in time burns down to a foundation of habitual resentment. Her first child, William, becomes the object of her passion to be served by romantic virility, and she makes the boy into a lady-killer whom she jealously adores. William dies while a young man, unable to venture farther in a life that was carrying him away from her, Lawrence implies. Paul, her third child, comes to prominence in the novel only after he is selected to replace the lost William in Mrs. Morel's erotic life.

Gertrude's power over her sons is fully convincing, for Lawrence presents her as a nonpareil. Beautiful in her youth, she retains her pleasing physical features and her engaging vitality into middle-age. Years of disillusionment and bitterness in her marriage cannot destroy her moral resilience or even her ready gaiety. Through most of the novel she wins the reader's sympathy because of her buoyant sense of identity with normative and vigorous natural life, her capacity for deeply imaginative response to experience, and her grace of ironic wit that suggests both instinctive modesty and intellectual intelligence.

All of these personal qualities are evident in her relations with her sons who delight in her company, and to Paul especially she becomes immeasurably attractive. But the reader, even while nostalgically valuing the portrayal of easy love between mother and child, is slowly unsettled by their spirited relations. Mrs. Morel misuses her sons's affections, and her maternal character is complicated by her unwittingly seductive, unfair advances upon his emotion. Pathetically, her unfulfilled vitality is expressed through an increasingly sexual love for Paul, who all through the novel cherishes an image of Gertrude as a lovely, creative, and buoyantly self-possessed woman. But the reader perceives even more clearly than the author, whose sympathy remains loyal to the mother, that Mrs. Morel becomes unprincipled and destructive in her jealous passion to keep Paul's love for herself.[8]

Sporadically, Paul's intelligence undermines his illusion of Gertrude by bringing him closer to conscious recognition of her real person and circumstances. While still a boy, he winces with pain whenever a situation reveals her too realistically as his aging mother instead of his glamorous mistress. Since most of the struggle in Paul's effort to achieve maturity and independence occurs at the obscure level of his emotions rather than in rational thought, the conflict between his illusion of Gertrude as his fantasy sweetheart and his active search for the reality of woman remains largely unconscious. The signs of his inner struggle are his displaced, symbolic actions toward other people, for any direct expression of either his love or his hostility toward his mother immediately defeats Paul with a backlash of anxiety or guilt. In the drama of Paul's unconsciousness, Miriam and Clara play Gertrude's role in disguise, as Daniel Weiss demonstrates in his study of *Sons and Lovers*.[9] Paul identifies both girls with his mother and he explores the errors and consequences of his illusion of her in his actual love affairs with them. The psychological and symbolic complexities of the novel do not undermine the realism of Paul's actions or the substantiality of any of the characters. *Sons and Lovers* is extraordinarily engaging even as a conventional novel with its vivid presentation of individuals and their social setting and the pathos of Paul's literal love-story; and this richness of objective material and explicit sentiment has made the book Lawrence's most widely appreciated work. But Lawrence's most significant achievement in this book is that he gives continuous narration to the deeply hidden life of Paul while maintaining the integrity of empirical facts that make up the fabric of the novel. Paul's relations with Miriam and Clara are literal, not allegorical, events; but it is also true that from the moment when he becomes his mother's favorite, the pattern of events in his life maintains an exact correlation between his unconscious attitudes toward Gertrude and his objective relations with his mistresses.

Paul and Miriam first meet in the chapter entitled "Death in the Family" (VI), just before Mrs. Morel in her bereavement over her older son transfers the full force of her possessive love onto Paul alone. At this moment of intensification in the mother-son relation, Miriam enters the fiction as a fully characterized counterpart to young, maidenly Gertrude, whose early description applies to them both: "She was still perfectly intact, deeply religious, and full of beautiful candour." (I) Like young Gertrude, Miriam is an intensely romantic girl, pietistic, something of an intellectual, and in a privately superior way she feels detached from her common circumstances. Like Gertrude, Miriam longs to be served by a virile hero, and she believes, rather bitterly as young Gertrude did, that being a man is everything. Most pertinently for Paul, probably, is Miriam's present degradation as the suffering servant of her boorish brothers. He sees her as she sees herself: an imprisoned princess turned swine-girl, deprived of her rightful chances in life. Paul's sympathy for the girl's situation is similar to the feeling he shares with his mother that her proper destiny was ruined by becoming a coal-miner's drudging wife. In order to preserve Gertrude's role as the idealized virgin-mother, Paul is capable of abusing Miriam relentlessly over any evidence of her abjection, dependency, and possessiveness, for he unconsciously associates these qualities with his mother's true character. In the Oedipal fantasy that would make his love all-powerful and exclusive, Paul wishes to countermand Gertrude's submission to another male by erasing the evidence of it from Miriam's reflection of his mother's image.

In Chapters VII and VIII Paul is unable even to attempt a sexual relation with Miriam because she corresponds too closely to the virginal mother of his fantasy whom he would protect or rescue from the evil male who has degraded her.

Because of this identification, Paul overemphasizes the inhibiting power of Miriam's maidenly and spiritual nature. He would in part prefer to keep his relation with Miriam as asexual as his relation with Gertrude ought to be. But as his sexual feelings are externalized and intensified by his romance with Miriam, Paul is trapped into openly battling his father over his erotic attachment to Gertrude. Walter Morel fails to defeat him and Paul virtually wins Gertrude as his own. (VIII) By Paul's unsought victory, Mrs. Morel's status changes in Paul's anxiety-ridden mind from the safe figure of the maidenly mother to the dangerous, sexually accessible figure of the untrue wife. His reaction to this change is to break off his romance with Miriam, telling her "you are a nun" (IX), and the careful reader is likely to be as shocked as Miriam by this misjudgment of her. By his abrupt rejection of the girl, Paul in his misery indicates his wish to reconstruct and fortify the barrier of sexual inhibition that had protected his relationship with the idealized Gertrude. He would like to enforce her desexualization, so that his usurpation of his father's place and the degradation of his mother might never have occurred. His distortion of Miriam is clearly willful, for Paul has all along been half-conscious that she does in fact recognize and want the male in him, as he somewhat abstractly says, but as long as Gertrude remained seemingly pure his sexual response toward Miriam was repressed and sufficiently ambiguous. After Gertrude's fall, however, Paul's view of Miriam is similarly altered merely by Clara's declaration of what has been obvious to everyone all along, that Miriam does indeed want him sexually. (X) He returns to Miriam with a sense of fate impelling him, and is able to woo her "now like a lover," Paul has emotionally painful sexual intercourse with her for a week, during which his heart is broken by his feeling of responsibility for having won and de-flowered the maiden figure whom he wished to revere as he wished to revere his mother. (XI)

The brief sexual episode keeps Paul at the point of crisis in his Oedipal tragedy, and he must come to some resolution of it. He abandons Miriam, and turns directly to Clara. (XII) With Clara no virginal aura reminiscent of his mother's former status interferes with his present response to fallen Woman as simply a sexual object; easily, he manages to leave her "out of count" and to deprive her of "respect," as she complains. (XIII) Because she does not seem pure to him, Paul's intercourse with her does not activate his *guilt* over the fact of his instinctual desire. Embracing her, he experiences the ecstatic relief of freely acknowledging his passion and he recognizes that his instinctual life is on the same innocent level as the life of nonhuman nature. But he cannot avoid the re-currence of his *anxiety*, or anticipation of retribution for his sexual license with another man's wife, especially since she symbolizes his mother whom he won in actual conflict with his father. Lawrence's own anxieties over this submerged drama are patently evident when it happens that Baxter Dawes, Clara's estranged but jealous husband, waylays Paul and badly beats him. The beating reinforces Paul's sense of his transgression, and he loses interest in Clara and begins to drift away from her. It is too late, however, to avert the catastro-phe. When Gertrude Morel and Baxter Dawes both fall seri-ously ill, Paul is terrified by this sudden prospect of the consequences of his deed. He suffers now because of what he fears that he was willfully done, but not because of what he feels that he essentially is.

Paul resumes his role as the loving and celibate son, dutiful toward both his stricken mother and the symbolic father-figure, to whom he feels grateful for having beaten him as his real father should have done to prevent the present trouble. (XIV) During the illnesses, Gertrude's physical degeneration and her bitterness against life nearly reveal her to Paul as the blameworthy person in their sexual crime; she becomes too explicitly a kind of overmastering hag. Tormented by a sense of complicity in her misery, Paul mixes a fatal dose of morphia into her cup of milk. (XIV) That this avowed mercy-killing actualizes Paul's unconscious desire to destroy his mother is shown by its analogue in his childhood conspiracy to sacrifice "Missis Arabella," as young Paul calls Annie's doll which he accidentally had broken.[10] The killing of Mrs. Morel not only reveals his wish to be free of her but also, with the simultaneity of neurotic behavior, his aggression dramatizes his compulsion to transgress all moral and psychic limitations in his attachment to her—especially since he elects to poison her and then wishes to suffocate her as she lies dying. The sexual overtones to the entire action rouse part of the feelings of horror and satisfaction in the episode.

With Gertrude dead, Paul resumes his devotion to her resurgent image as an eternally lovely, innocent maiden. (XV) To erase the evidence that their fantasy-affair was symbolically consummated, he returns her surrogate, Clara, to a happy reconciliation with Baxter, for whom he develops great affection as he helps nurse the stricken man back to health. (XIV) Paul's attempts to reconstruct an illusional past of normal family relations are of course pathetic failures to accept the demonstrated facts of his mother's life and character or to recognize his own continuing bondage to her. But he has strengthened his will and ability to survive her, in spite of his grief. Paul is able to turn toward life because in his gratifying sexual experience with Clara he learned to associate his sexual being with the life of benign nature. Paul's attachment to the values of nature and creativity enables him to inherit the role of a life-bearer that Gertrude filled earlier in the novel, when she displayed stoical self-sufficiency in spite of her oppressive circumstances. The fiction's representation of Gertrude as a creative vessel fades when Paul, through the "baptism of fire in passion," acquires the aura of unconscious vitality that was Gertrude's glory—but in the end is his.

The novel is structured by these several transpositions of personal roles and symbolic episodes that culminate in Paul's identification with the fantasy-image of his mother. Gertrude's death completes his mythic conception of her as a lovely, creative maiden ravaged by her coarse, relentless fate; and in love with his Persephone, he embraces the positive values that she represented in life.[11] His deliberative, artistic sensibility and his devotion to the vitality of unconscious nature are associated with her femininity. The woman at the back of Paul Morel is more than the idealized memory of his mother; the feminine image is identified with his essential self. His final rejection of marriage with Miriam, in a labored episode that is superfluous to the narrative, signals his complete internalization of the reality of woman. He does not need Miriam or Clara either; but he clearly will need to learn to identify with a man, or else to seek man's love effeminately. Paul's only commitment of feeling in the latter part of the novel is his new friendship with his attacker, Baxter Dawes, toward whom he displays self-effacing, gentle affection.

For Lawrence, who went on to live the adventure that Paul approaches, the confusion of sexual roles remained critical in his development as an artist. His creative self was so closely bound to his image of woman that he needed constantly to defend the genius of himself against the conscious shame of effeminacy. As an artist he usually remained true to that delicate sensitiveness which he noted in women, but he felt undermined as a man in society and threatened as a sexual being by his sense of femininity. He adopted a bearded appearance like his father's, he prided himself on having a quarrelsome temperament, and he often voiced the authoritarian ideals of a fierce masculinity that did not accurately reflect his own deeper nature. It was nearly impossible for Lawrence to identify casually and satisfactorily with men because the psychological tragedies of his childhood family life gave him a notion of manliness that offered no love and invited none from him. The unsatisfied need for masculine identification enters all of Lawrence's works, in which he pursues an ideal of maleness that he could never recognize in the circumstantial world and that his own divided nature could never wholly accept. He proposed sacred fellowships at every level of man's experience, from "eternal" friendships to impassioned national parties and occult priesthoods. In his most ambitious efforts at self-integration, he tried to reorganize whole societies or to imagine new ones in which his feelings and gifts would not appear inconsistent with manly powers. His ambivalence toward both male and female roles led him into preternaturally sensitive examinations of all human relations and institutions in his effort to find a habitable world for the individual soul that strides, like Paul Morel, away from psychological oppression and death toward spontaneous participation in external reality. In this quest for psychic freedom, Lawrence's personal psychology becomes manifest in his involvement with actual places in the world. He projected his feelings onto "England," and when the actual England failed to become what he desired, he continued to explore his own reality by projecting it onto other countries, other places, other settings in his works, that promise or fail to suit his requirements for self-realization.

3

"There must be a new world"

When the first reviews of *Sons and Lovers* were drawing attention to Lawrence's work and bringing him some acclaim, he and Frieda returned briefly to London so that she might visit her children. During these weeks in the middle of 1913 Lawrence met several of the people who later figured prominently in his life and who influenced the development of his ideas and his art. The chief new acquaintances were John Middleton Murry and Katherine Mansfield, who were living together and editing a little magazine, through which Lawrence had come to know about them. At this time he also met Edward Marsh, an influential patron of writers, who as an editor had published Lawrence in *Georgian Poetry*. Through Marsh, who was also a high ranking Secretary in the Admiralty, the "Lawrences," as they pretended to be, were introduced to Herbert Asquith and his wife, Lady Cynthia, the son and daughter-in-law of the Prime Minister. This introduction too was "a tremendous success," as Marsh reported, and Cynthia Asquith remained a major figure in Lawrence's experience.

The growth of a broader social context for the writer continued during the following summer when Lawrence and Frieda again returned from Italy to England after Frieda's divorce was granted, intending to remain in London only to be married. At that time, Lawrence met Catherine Carswell, a reviewer and biographer who remained his unwavering and selfless defender in all his literary broils. Lawrence also became acquainted with Samuel Koteliansky, a translator and journalist who joined the intimate circle around the Lawrence-Murry friendship. It was while on a walking tour with "Kot" that Lawrence learned of the outbreak of war in August 1914. The companions were unusually carefree and had been cavorting their way through the countryside, Lawrence dancing with water-lilies twisted around his hat and Kot intoning a favorite Hebrew psalm that calls holy men to celebrate the Lord, when they entered a village and were stunned by the news of war and by the first mad chauvinism of the civilian population. From that moment, Lawrence was trapped once more in England, for the duration of the conflict.

He was deeply upset by the prospect of total European warfare, and what he called "the ghastliness and mechanical, obsolete, hideous stupidity of war" made him generally bitter against human beings. "I have never come so near to hating mankind as I am now," he wrote in September; and one recognizes with a sense of the fact's curious implications that Lawrence had indeed never come near to misanthropy before this shock to his expectations of fundamental good will among mankind. Even in the same letter, he modifies his bitterness with a word of general encouragement to Gordon Campbell, who was in marital difficulty: "It isn't one's *conscious* self that matters so much. We are conscious mad. But at the back of it all, we are sane and healthy and original." (*CL* 290–91) He tried to maintain a happy view of basic human nature even in the face of the war, by explaining the conflict as the European soul's desperate revolt against a false set of values. The materialism of present civilization, he argued, diverts a man from his proper self-realization and binds him to the deathly purpose of economic gain. In a "Study of Thomas Hardy," written in the fall of 1914 and acknowledged as a *"confessio fidei,"* Lawrence tried to construe the war as a fight for psychic freedom:

> It is a war for freedom of the bonds of our own coward-ice and sluggish greed of security and well-being; it is a fight to regain ourselves out of the grip of our caution. . . . We are, every one of us, revelling at this moment in the squandering of human life as if it were something we needed. And it is shameful. And all because that, to *live*, we are afraid to risk ourselves. We can only die. . . . If you or I die, it will not matter, so long as there is alive in the land some new sense of what is and what is not, some new courage to let go the securities, and to *be*, to risk ourselves in a forward venture of life, as we are willing to risk ourselves in death. (P 407-8)

With civilization apparently breaking down, Lawrence felt that it was more urgent than ever to proclaim the naturally good part of man and strengthen it against the moral disinte-gration of the times. With the Murrys and Kot, Lawrence projected plans for a little colony where about twenty sensi-tive, creative souls could protectively live together in harmony and independence. The utopian idea of Rananim—Lawrence coined the name from the opening Hebrew words of Kot's psalm (Psalm XXXIII), *Ranenu tzadikim*—took shape during the winter and Christmas season of 1914. The colony was to be established on some unpopulated island where they would go as soon as the war ended: maybe in the southern oceans, maybe off South America, maybe near Australia. Finally

Katherine Mansfield caused Lawrence bitter chagrin by gathering up maps and asking him to pinpoint a specific location. Under her jeering challenge, he remained silent that night.

The war did not end in a few months, as they were hoping. As the nations entrenched, Lawrence vacillated between his plans for a utopian break from society and a plan for the social reconstruction of England, sometimes considering both concurrently and with equal enthusiasm. A new group of influential acquaintances acquired in early 1915 certainly supported the possibility of Lawrence "doing something" within England. He was lionized briefly by Lady Ottoline Morrell, an active social figure who moved freely among bohemians and aristocrats, and who influenced her husband to take his pacifist stand in Parliament. Through Lady Ottoline, Lawrence met Bertrand Russell, even then a political activist and a pacifist in regard to the war. For a while the hope of Lawrence's new world seemed to lie in England. By February 1 his conversations with Lady Ottoline brought Lawrence to the edge of beatific anticipation:

> I must write you a line when you have gone, to tell you how my heart feels quite big with hope for the future. Almost with the remainder of tears and the last gnashing of teeth, I could sing the *Magnificat* for the child in my heart.
>
> I want you to form the nucleus of a new community which shall start a new life amongst us—a life in which the only riches is integrity of character. So that each one may fulfil his own nature and deep desires to the utmost, but wherein tho', the ultimate satisfaction and joy is in the completeness of us all as one. Let us be good all together, instead of just in the privacy of our chambers, let us know that the intrinsic part of all of us is the best part, the believing part, the passionate, generous part. We can all come croppers, but what does it mat-

ter? We can laugh at each other, and dislike each other, but the good remains and we know it. And the new community shall be established upon the known, eternal good part in us. This present community consists, as far as it is a framed thing, in a myriad contrivances for preventing us from being let down by the meanness in ourselves or in our neighbors. . . . It is no good plastering and tinkering with this community. Every strong soul must put off its connection with this society, its vanity and chiefly its fear, and go naked with its fellows, weaponless, armourless, without shield or spear, but only with naked hands and open eyes. Not self-sacrifice, but fulfilment, the flesh and the spirit in league together not in arms against one another. And each man shall know that he is part of the greater body. (CL 311–12)

In May, Lawrence wrote to Cynthia Asquith: "We in England shall unite in our knowledge of God to live according to the best of our knowledge, Prime Ministers and Capitalists and artisans all working in pure effort towards God—here, tomorrow, in this England." (CL 343) This spirit of hope affected even the *realpolitiker* Frieda, who assured Kot that "our Rananim will come off in some form or other"; but she brooded over whether Lawrence could achieve more with his important new friends if he did not have an outspoken German wife.

With Russell, Lawrence began preparing a series of lectures they would give together, Russell discussing ethics and Lawrence speaking on immortality. He planned to rent a hall in London and have Lady Ottoline preside at the public meetings, and the band of believers themselves would have their headquarters at Garsington, the Morrells' estate. But by July, Lawrence had quarreled violently with Russell and the lectures were doomed. Their disagreement arose over Russell's reluctance, or inability, to present speculative schemes for a

radically new society, and Lawrence's obstreperous insistence
that mere criticism of present flaws was by itself worse than
pointless. Russell seemed to be just plastering and tinkering,
and Lawrence looked forward to something like a Jerusalem
in England's pleasant land. After this proposed venture failed,
Lawrence and the Murrys intended to scatter seeds of new
moral thought with a little magazine, *The Signature*, but it
had to be abandoned after three issues for lack of subscrip-
tions. Lawrence wrote bitterly to Lady Cynthia about the
supercilious attitude people were taking toward his hopes for
a better world:

> I've got a real bitterness in my soul, just now, as if
> Russell and Lady Ottoline were traitors—they are trai-
> tors. They betray the real truth. They come to me, and
> they make me talk, and they enjoy it, it gives them a
> profoundly gratifying sensation. And that is all. As if
> what I say were meant only to give them gratification,
> because of the flavour of personality, as if I were a cake
> or a wine or a pudding. Then they say I, D. H. L., am
> wonderful, I am an exceedingly valuable personality,
> and that the things I say are extravaganzas, illusions.
> They say I cannot think. (*CL* 362)

There is, clearly, the flavor of personality in Lawrence's expectation of utopian changes in England, and at this point in
his life he did not bother to think carefully about economic
or political problems. His impatience and vagueness about
programmatic details, which he dismissed as "temporal
things," evade any practical application of his vision; his only
specific recommendations were made in a self-confident letter
to Russell during the heyday of their mutual regard:

> There must be a revolution in the state. It shall begin
> by the nationalising of all industries and means of com-
> munication, and of the land—in one fell blow. Then a

man shall have his wages whether he is sick or well or old—if anything prevents his working, he shall have his wages just the same. So we shall not live in fear of the wolf—no man amongst us, and no woman, shall have any fear of the wolf at the door, for all wolves are dead.

Which practically solves the whole economic question for the present. All dispossessed owners shall receive a proportionate income—no capital recompense—for the space of, say fifty years. (*CL* 317)

One sympathizes with those who discounted Lawrence's ideas. This cavalierly voiced proposal was supposed to stir the convictions of the analytically minded Russell—who was at the time familiar with the complexities of economics as viewed by his friend John Maynard Keynes.[1]

Economic reorganization, which was only the minor substructure of Lawrence's social vision, became a major public issue in postwar England, and Lawrence's revolutionary ideas of 1915 vaguely anticipate the later proposals of reform. Among the resolutions of the newly vitalized Labour Party in 1918 were demands for the nationalization of land and industry and for a guaranteed minimum wage, but it is unlikely that Lawrence had any understanding of the actual complexities of these measures or that he was interested in the programs of socialists or the Labourites beyond the coincidence of a few general principles on his part. It should be noted that the Labourites themselves were unable to effect any part of their program until the 1940's.[2]

But during his disappointments as a political activist Lawrence's principal effort was the completion of *The Rainbow*, his most lyrical and visionary novel; and it is clear that his concurrent attempt to lead a social movement arose from the overflowing passion of his creative work. Lawrence appears

naïve when he ardently proclaims a new world to his Bloomsbury acquaintances and to a society in wartime, but he was
acting from his deepest commitment at the moment to a
utopian vision which he pursued with finer awareness in the
novel. In *The Rainbow* Lawrence maintains a utopian attitude toward the future, but his representation of present life
reveals that most men's souls are hopelessly divided by conflicting passions that seem innate, and that man's griefs do not
arise solely from industrialism or specifically modern circumstances of life. His optimism about man's nature is modified
and corrected against the concreteness of the fiction.

The Rainbow is the history of three generations in the
Brangwen family. Each Brangwen protagonist struggles
against the limits of farm or village life and reaches for a
wider range of personal experience in society and with ideas.
The movement toward a wider circle of life suggests at all
times its possibly tragic futility, for the goals of social mobil-
ity and intellectual awareness are achieved at the expense of
deep sensual vigor that seems to be sustained only by rural life
and family, or generic, uniformity. But each protagonist
pushes life a tiny bit forward toward new possibilities of total
human fulfillment before he or she lapses into the stability and
decay of his personal limit and the self-confinement of his
achieved social identity. Even though individuals largely fail
in their personal goals, the promise of human success is kept
alive and extended by each generation, and the novel ends
with an ecstatic suggestion of what the future can be for common mankind.

In the opening pages a highly generalized view of the
Brangwen ancestors presents as in a pre-curtain episode, or a
dumb-show, the social and psychological situation that will
influence the history: like Fate that curbs and spurs all indi-

vidualism. Nameless, vaguely characterized Brangwen men
live in close, unthinking contact with the order of natural life
as they work their farms, and they feel their strength replen-
ished by sharing the vitality that lifts the grain and moves the
animals. Their womenfolk, however, are weary of heavy
work, resentful of their solitude and the early loss of youth.
They look beyond the farm to the horizon where the church
steeple and the town signify opportunities for self-
development and more vivid, more varied experience. The
narrative maintains this dialectical polarity between the instinctual and the conscious requirements for life, and the
struggle toward a synthesis of perfectly integrated human-
kind continues for three generations. Pairs of lovers marry
and find that their psychological differences heal or aggravate
the internal conflicts that afflict them as separate persons.

The generations incur greater difficulties in their lives as the
family moves from the farm into the village and on to middle-
class urban life. Though the individuals fare better economi-
cally and gain sophistication, their dissatisfactions increase as
they separate themselves from the norms of nonhuman nature, where passion and beauty are the strengths of life. In the
third generation the heroine, Ursula, finds her soul utterly degraded by the ugliness of her industrial civilization and by its
subversion of a person's sensual vitality. At the conclusion, her
uncertain future indicates the unsettled but hopeful destiny of
all her lineage who lifted their energies to a higher level of
experience.

Like all the Brangwens before her, she represents not only
her personal self but also a family type or subpersonal being
that is elevated from the level of undifferentiated natural creatures to that of troubled individuals in a world of men. Lawrence focuses attention on the varied but consanguineous

qualities of the Brangwen soul by softening the lines which separate one personal identity from another. Through the first half of the novel we know little about the appearance, mannerisms, or gestures of the major characters. The outlines of their identities are left dim, and the matrix of human consciousness flows from person to person. Ian Watt's study, *The Rise of the Novel*, demonstrates that the individuation of characters in the traditional English novel depends chiefly on the specificity of time and space dimensions for the particularized details which define individuals from the mass of mankind.[3] Lawrence, however, like Paul Morel trying to paint the shimmering protoplasm within a leaf, subdues dimensional features in order to accentuate his characters' unconscious vitality. When Tom Brangwen, the protagonist in the first generation, decides that he must marry Lydia Lensky, a Polish widow with a small daughter, Lawrence employs a method of generalized narration for the entire development. Time and space dimensions are so vaguely given that the actions and thoughts of the characters are not attached to specifically detailed settings, circumstances, or moments of consciousness.[4] By avoiding the data of specific mental impressions, Lawrence directs attention to Tom's and Lydia's subrational impulses to love that prevail in them both despite their contrary currents of revulsion:

> Sometimes her vagueness, in which he was lost, made him angry, made him rage. But he held himself still as yet. She had no response, no being towards him. It puzzled and enraged him, but he submitted for a long time. Then, from the accumulated troubling of her ignoring him, gradually a fury broke out, destructive, and he wanted to go away, to escape her.
>
> It happened she came down to the Marsh with the child whilst he was in this state. Then he stood over

against her, strong and heavy in his revolt, and though he said nothing, still she felt his anger and heavy impatience grip hold of her, she was shaken again as out of a torpor. Again her heart stirred with a quick, out-running impulse, she looked at him, at the stranger who was not a gentleman yet who insisted on coming into her life, and the pain of a new birth in herself strung all her veins to a new form. She would have to begin again, to find a new being, a new form, to respond to that blind, insistent figure standing over against her.

A shiver, a sickness of new birth passed over her, the flame leaped up him, under his skin. She wanted it, this new life from him, with him, yet she must defend herself against it, for it was a destruction.

As he worked alone on the land, or sat up with his ewes at lambing time, the facts and material of his daily life fell away, leaving the kernel of his purpose clean. And then it came upon him that he would marry her and she would be his life. (I)

From the first quoted sentence, the action continues within a general time scheme, "Sometimes . . . then . . . ." It is repeated in the sequence, "It happened she . . . Then he . . . ." The implication of repeated, lingering or habitual responses is strengthened by Lawrence's grammatical devices such as the suggestion of imperfect tense—"as he worked"— and subjunctive mood—"for it was a destruction." He usually predicates a state of action rather than a discrete act: "he held himself still as yet," "he stood over against her," "she must defend herself." In the second paragraph the action is transferred to Brangwen's Marsh Farm, but there are still no spatial details which would fix a setting and moment for the psychic drama between the characters. The episode is not dramatically presented in the ordinary, objective way; that is, we do not *see* a hand's unconscious movement or *hear* a curious tone of voice. The drama remains mostly internal, as in the final paragraph when Tom at some indefinite time realizes his decisive desire. Throughout this example, the narrative develops without the particularity that defines personal motives and specific feelings.

Lawrence carefully explained the purpose of this method in a letter to Garnett when the novel was still in its formative stage during Lawrence's second sojourn in Italy. Garnett objected to the characterization in the version of the manuscript that he read, and though Lawrence later rewrote his book his defense of his first version clarifies what he intended and accomplished in the end. "I don't think the psychology is wrong," he answered Garnett; "it is only that I have a different attitude to my characters, and that necessitates a different attitude in you, which you are not prepared to give." Lawrence found it hard to explain the rationale of his unconventional methods, but he took support from the current idiom of the Futurists, whose poetry and paintings and essays he encountered in Italy.[5] Their interest in realizing "an intuitive physiology of matter" made Lawrence think that his new book was "a bit futuristic," for he was trying to realize the physiology not of matter but of being: "that which is physic —non-human, in humanity, is more interesting to me than the old-fashioned human element."

> I don't so much care about what the woman *feels*—in the ordinary usage of the word. That presumes an *ego* to feel with. I only care about what the woman *is*—what she IS—inhumanly, physiologically, materially—according to the use of the word: but for me, what she *is* as a phenomenon (or as representing some greater, inhuman will), instead of what she feels according to the human conception. . . . You mustn't look in my novel for the old stable *ego*—of the character. There is

another *ego*, according to whose action the individual is unrecognisable, and passes through, as it were, allotropic states which it needs a deeper sense than any we've been used to exercise, to discover are states of the same single radically unchanged element. (Like as diamond and coal are the same pure single element of carbon. "Diamond, what! This is carbon." And my diamond might be coal or soot, and my theme is carbon.) You must not say my novel is shaky—it is not perfect, because I am not expert in what I want to do. But it is the real thing, say what you like. And I shall get my reception, if not now, then before long. Again I say, don't look for the development of the novel to follow the lines of certain characters: the characters fall into the form of some other rhythmic form, as when one draws a fiddle-bow across a fine tray delicately sanded, the sand takes lines unknown. (*CL* 281–82)

One of the allotropic states of Tom Brangwen's soul is his desire to marry, and we see that his decision emerges from underneath his conscious mind. It is partly but not merely his sexual need that directs him. Lydia is a romantic mystery to him, and part of his desire for her is his Brangwen will ("some greater, inhuman will") to extend life into unknown areas. From his first attraction to her, he felt "a curious certainty about her, as if she were destined to him. It was to him a profound satisfaction that she was a foreigner." After their marriage Lydia's firm and mysterious separateness that roused him, and which he still values, continues intermittently to irritate him. She loses herself in thought about her past life, or she becomes fully absorbed with maternal cares, while Tom waits, sometimes bitterly, to be admitted again to her life. In the second year, they achieve a union that surpasses their earlier knowledge of each other: "it was the baptism to another life, it was the complete confirmation. . . . The new world was discovered, it remained only to be explored." Even then, their indissoluble relation modifies but does not destroy their separate identities, and under the arch of their consummation in marriage the small child, Anna, grows up as if under the pillars of a rainbow: "Her father and mother now met to the span of the heavens, and she, the child, was free to play in the space beneath, between." (III)

The story of Anna Lensky, Tom's stepdaughter, takes the foreground of the fiction as she falls in love and marries her cousin, Will Brangwen. In their season of courting, they gather up sheaves one moonlit night and they realize their passion for each other as they accumulate one great shock of wheat. The tension of their sexual attraction builds slowly through four pages of narrative that is developed by the changing aspect of the setting itself, for Lawrence describes the wheat field in a symbolic way that makes the scene convey the drama of the episode. The moon flaring over the field becomes more luminous, more pervasive, changing the colors and proportions of the natural objects. Anna truly forgets herself in her entranced subjection to the beauty of the moment, and her own mind is unable to tell us anything about her. Lawrence cannot write *she thought this* or *she felt that*, because she has entered a state of purely sensual consciousness. She sees the world with heightened reference to her state of desire, and her relation to the symbolic scene gives the reader insight to the underlying causality of her actions. By contrast, Will's worrisome, self-conscious incapacity to lose his thoughts under the influence of the looming natural images indicates the constrained mentalism of his character that will prevent his fulfillment in marriage. For Anna, the physical setting glows with the energy of love, and Lawrence makes all the natural world a continuous and varied extension of her inner state as the lovers finally embrace:

> "My love!" she called, in a low voice, from afar. The low sound seemed to call to him from far off, under the moon, to him who was unaware. He stopped, quivered, and listened.
>
> "My love," came again the low, plaintive call, like a bird unseen in the night. (IV)

Anna is represented in terms which support a sense of extensive place: "from afar," "from far off, under the moon," "came again," "like a bird unseen in the night"—while Will is the static figure within her emotional landscape: "seemed to call to him," "to him who was unaware. He stopped, quivered, and listened." Yet during this moment they have been in each other's arms. The setting we have been most directly aware of is metaphorical and is not composed of real space. The human states of being are represented as forms in nature. The actual scene disappears from the world of things and appearances to become integrated with the deepest level of Anna's subjectivity—and because the setting is a strikingly romantic, healthy, and fecund portion of earth, a good deal of cheery inference about Anna automatically accompanies this method of identification.

They go to live in the village of Cossethay, and their honeymoon begins blissfully. During his holiday from work, Will is astonished by the power of Anna's love to create a new world for them apart from other people and utterly free of "the established rule of things" in the daylit, workaday world outside their cottage. He is troubled a little "in his orderly, conventional mind" to see his experience altered so abruptly, but:

he let her do as she liked with him, and shone with
strange pleasure. She was to dispose of him as she would.
He was translated with gladness to be in her hands. And
down went his qualms, his maxims, his rules, his smaller
beliefs, she scattered them like an expert skittle-player.
He was very much astonished and delighted to see them
scatter. (VI)

Marriage temporarily gives Will the sense that his experience is eternally fixed and ultimately fulfilling. But suddenly,
Anna threatens to take his new world away from him as easily
and abruptly as she created it. In her happy indifference to ul-
timates of any sort, Anna decides to give a tea-party, and Will
is angered by this reintroduction of the common, objective
world within their lives. Ashamed of his dependence on her,
he burns with hatred for her, and they turn violently against
each other as they resume their separate roles and various relationships. Unlike the older couple in their daily life on the
farm, Will cannot help himself psychically and Anna cannot
easily forget her resentment of his rages. Their early marital
battles are murderous; one of them lasts two days and fills five
pages with seething misery:

> His hovering near her, wanting her to be with him,
> the futility of him, the way his hands hung, irritated her
> beyond bearing. She turned on him blindly and destruc-
> tively, he became a mad creature, black and electric
> with fury. The dark storms rose in him, his eyes glowed
> black and evil, he was fiendish in his thwarted soul.
>
> There followed two black and ghastly days, when she
> was set in anguish against him, and he felt as if he were
> in a black, violent underworld, and his wrists quivered
> murderously. And she resisted him. He seemed a dark,
> almost evil thing, pursuing her, hanging on to her, bur-
> dening her. She would give anything to have him
> removed.

"You need some work to do," she said. "You ought to be at work. Can't you *do* something?"

His soul only grew the blacker. His condition now became complete, the darkness of his soul was thorough. Everything had gone: he remained complete in his own tense, black will. He was now unaware of her. She did not exist. His dark, passionate soul had recoiled upon itself, and now, clinched and coiled round a centre of hatred, existed in its own power. There was a curiously ugly pallor, an expressionlessness in his face. She shuddered from him. She was afraid of him. His will seemed grappled upon her. (VI)

Sensual experience in marriage is too unpredictable, too contradictory to support Will's sense of life's value and purpose. He cannot submit to the death of his rigid conceptions of love, just as he cannot easily accept changes in his experience. Bitterly he comes to destroy his unfinished woodcarving of Eve: he cannot finish it, for although marriage with Anna breaks down his counterfeit notion of woman, he is unable to praise the reality. Will seeks transcendent experience and fixed ideals through spiritual piety. When he and Anna visit Lincoln Cathederal he is ecstatic amidst the visible triumph of spirit over the limitations of flesh and stone. To him the church is an image of spiritualized woman—as his unfinished woodcarving had been. The cathedral arch symbolizes unslacking ecstasy, the intense and timeless pleasure which the first days of marriage had been for him. But Anna again ejects him from his Eden by forcing him to recognize the odd little faces carved in stone that are like mementos of what the cathedral arch does not express. Their impish, sly expressions celebrate the holy comedy of the temporal, physical world that to Anna is the only real one. She mocks and spoils his simple reverence for the Lamb as a symbol of holiness.

Anna herself is a lioness—and Will is the first to perceive the resemblance as she sits happily in bed on the morning after their wedding, her mane of brown hair sticking out round her face and her dark eyes, her nose sniffing forward over the breakfast tray. She can unfold the depths of herself with a natural creature's fierce vitality that Will cannot match. He loves her sometimes brutally in order to dominate her and assert his will, but she conquers him at his own game, turning her sharpness against his pretense of mastership, and in sex she often leaves him satiated but bewildered.

When the children begin to arrive, Anna gives herself joyously to motherhood and she learns to be gentler with her husband, to placate his black temper and accommodate him, for which he is grateful and humble toward her. But she remains the creator and leader in this life together. Anna is "Anna Victrix," blithe, freely responding to experience, grateful for life. The disappointments and oppression of marriage and domestic routine distress her only briefly; the possibility of an even richer experience than hers fades from her thoughts, and she gathers the edges of the symbolic horizon about herself. "With satisfaction she relinquished the adventure to the unknown." The rainbow is the sun and moon that span her day. "She was a door and a threshold, she herself." (VI) She has unfolded and ripened in life and her personal vividness in episodes of both joy and strife is treated in the novel as a triumph over the grief and the false ideology that would degrade her soul.

In her generation she is the fiction's life-bearer, and her succession to her parents' glory is explicitly signaled by the repetitions of basic patterns and images of experience in both generations. The transpositions of personal roles and symbolic episodes that structure this novel are an elaboration of the structural principle of *Sons and Lovers*. In *The Rainbow* the method is more consciously designed and rhythmically sustained. One Brangwen protagonist gives way to another in the ordinary course of a family history; and a great many rainbows, moons, and far horizons reappear in symbolic contexts unifying the saga of three generations with recurrent signs of their fulfillment, sensual vitality, and expanding life.

But Anna's success differs from her parents' mutual achievement. She is only one person drawing fulfillment from a marriage, and her "victory" leaves Will broken in his shell of idealism. Will lives in strange misery that becomes evident in his appearance:

> As he sat sometimes very still, with a bright, vacant face, Anna could see the suffering among the brightness. He was aware of some limit to himself, of something unformed in his very being, of some buds which were not ripe in him, some folded centres of darkness which would never develop and unfold whilst he was alive in the body. He was unready for fulfillment. Something undeveloped in him limited him, there was a darkness in him which he could not unfold, which would never unfold in him. (VII)

The extraordinary repetitiveness of this passage emphasizes Will's inability to give form and expression to his true individual nature. Through Will's story, Lawrence dwells on the effects of unfulfillment in the male character. Even after the narrative focuses on the children in the third generation, Lawrence returns to the parents' fate to show that some inchoate desire of Will's soul degenerates into mechanistic lust, and he comes to Anna for a last frenzy of "gratification":

> This was what their love had become, a sensuality violent and extreme as death. They had no conscious inti-

macy, no tenderness of love. It was all the lust and the infinite, maddening intoxication of the sense, a passion of death. (VIII)

Will's earlier sense of physical shame becomes part of his "extreme delight" in voluptuousness. He at last becomes an active soul but only in the violence of pure lust as he perfects unsurpassable sensations in his contacts with Anna's body. From his sexual frenzy a new man emerges to become a pillar —not of the rainbow, but of the community. He begins to feel responsibility for public affairs, and he becomes an exponent of crafts instruction in the public schools. In his mature years he is the organist for the church, and he is the teacher of crafts for the town's boys. His reduction into a machine for sexual sensations coincides with his new activity as a minor public figure, who stands up for social progress and traditional institutions. The implication, which is sustained through the remainder of the novel, is that these developments in Will occur with a similar correlation in modern civilization generally. The material and intellectual achievements of the twentieth century are linked by Lawrence to the decadence of man's sensual energy that can find no natural fulfillment. Englishmen of power and success in the world are represented in the last half of the novel as inwardly disfigured types.

The supreme task of Brangwen self-realization falls to Ursula. The second half of the novel carries her through the broadest range of social and private experience as, in her growth from childhood to young womanhood, she vacillates between the guides of convention and the dictates of her deep self. In Ursula's life the crises of the Brangwen destiny are all met before and outside of a formal marriage relation; her singleness surpasses even her mother's, but the cost of maintaining her integrity is greater for her and it postpones her maturation in marriage. She is the novel's twentieth-century person: easily freed from limiting material circumstances and consciously aspiring to self-fulfillment, yet deprived of adequate support within her family or social role, Ursula is directly exposed to all the powerful stimuli and corrosions of modern life.

As a self-absorbed and romantically inclined girl, Ursula suffers from being the oldest child in a teeming household, and her plight amidst the clamor of babies and interfering brothers and sisters is one of the winning episodes of domestic comedy in the novel, matched only by the earlier festivity of her parents' wedding. Ursula's longing for spiritual exaltation and her fantasies of ideal love and stately glamor (she avidly reads *The Idylls of the King*) are part of the vanity of a young girl's self-articulation. When she is allowed to take the train each day for grammar school at Nottingham, Ursula begins to believe that the course of events may in actuality rescue her from the narrow domesticity that she abhors in her mother's life. When she is sent to high school she feels that she is becoming a lady. Much of the acquired gentility, however, proves oppressive, and she learns in her adolescent "first love" for Anton Skrebensky that what is refined in the social sense is neither exhilarating nor liberating. Though Anton is associated with her grandmother's aristocratic Polish background, and though he is a romantic young officer in the Army Engineers, he lacks a natural vitality that Ursula recognizes in the glance and sensitivity of a common bargeman. Anton's vocation as a soldier strikes her as a stiff outward shape that hides the hollowness of soul within him. But girlishly, she sentimentalizes their love when Anton must return to duty.

Her growth into a woman of balanced sensual and intellectual development includes an attachment to her lesbian school instructor, whose caresses soothe her hypersensitive body. Eventually she feels revulsion for the affair, and she designedly introduces Winifred to her Uncle Tom, a colliery manager. Overseeing the pits at Wiggiston, the younger Tom Brangwen revels in what he reviles, serving the machine that dehumanizes the colliers and makes the squalid town a monstrous side show to the mechanisms of industry. He and Winifred soon marry, with Lawrence's sardonic blessing: "She would make him a good companion. She was his mate."

Ursula fights her parents for the freedom to have a job teaching school, and in her authoritarian role as a school mistress she learns the mortification of being an operative in the machine of society. After two years of bullying and being bullied, she flies to her opportunity to take a degree at the university, where for a while she is inspired by intellectual exertion before becoming disillusioned by the lifelessness of scientific ideas and theories.

The crisis in Ursula's effort to be fully herself occurs in her renewed love for Skrebensky—that is accountable only because the romance is fated formally by its many parallels with the experience of the previous two generations. Skrebensky returns on a six months' leave after six years away in Africa, and immediately they declare their continuing love for each other. After a few weeks of reblossoming romance they have sexual intercourse under a great oak tree during the roaring of a night wind in spring. This consummation, which takes place under the pagan symbol accompanied by the empathetic passion of nature, vindicates Ursula's soul—just as Paul Morel felt vindicated by his "baptism of passion." But Skrebensky cannot for very long sustain his passion on the level of Ursula's direct identification with a natural world of rudimentary symbols. He cannot follow her revocation of "the ordinary mortal world," for that world is the source of his only developed identity, his social role. He wants to marry Ursula, to give some social organization to their love, and to take her to India on his next military assignment. Swayed, Ursula agrees. But at a weekend party on the coast he fails to match her in self-forgetting sexual sympathy with the heaving, infinite sea and the round bright moon; and as a result of the bitter, shaming failure of that episode Skrebensky readily accepts the end of their engagement.

When Ursula recuperates from a feverish illness following a miscarriage, she senses that she has finally cast off the last husk and shell of outward life and that she will travel into the future as a firm, beautifully flowering individual. As she lies convalescing in the family's new brick house in a colliery town, her situation symbolizes the imminent rebirth of vitality in tested and healed individuals who will rise free of the materialism and corruption of the social world. Her faith is confirmed in the reappearance of a rainbow over the countryside, and she looks to a millennial era for all mankind.

Ursula's maturely joyous independence is a happy ending which the reader steadily anticipates in spite of all the unhappiness in the Brangwensaga. The structural and symbolic devices of the novel build up a rhythmic movement of recurrent promises and partial achievements of individual fulfillment that point to a glorious Brangwen destiny and suggest its extension through all society. The momentum allows the author's personal hope to set the tone on every page, and the tone cushions each distressing episode against despairing inferences that might be drawn from each of the partial failures. The double viewpoint toward the story keeps the author's presence obvious in the signs of his doubting and affirming participation in the fiction. Concurrently damning and glorifying his characters, Lawrence's method is a perfectly sustained formal quality of the novel; and it justifies the emergence of his own voice in the conclusion to announce Ursula's vision of the future: [6]

> And the rainbow stood on the earth. She knew that the sordid people who crept hard-scaled and separate on the face of the world's corruption were living still, that the rainbow was arched in their blood and would quiver to life in their spirit, that they would cast off their horny covering of disintegration, that new, clean, naked bodies would issue to a new germination, to a new growth, rising to the light and the wind and the clean rain of heaven. She saw in the rainbow the earth's new architecture, the old, brittle corruption of houses and factories swept away, the world built up in a living fabric of Truth, fitting to the over-arching heaven. (XVI)

The concluding vision, like the opening dumb-show by the Brangwen ancestors, speaks of human life in vague metaphors of vegetative growth: bodies cast off their coverings, germinate, issue, rise to the light and rain. The diction refocuses our lasting attention on man's unconscious, bodily energy that is the natural force of health and creation. The natural human being is also associated with animal imagery in the novel, as with the farm animals of the opening chapters, or with the aggressive birds and beasts that are images for the marital conflict in the second generation, or with the rampaging horses in Ursula's fevered delirum. But it is chiefly the landscape that defines what is basic and "good" in human nature. The landscape glows or fades throughout the novel as the major characters gain or lose a capacity for symbolic vision that relates their objective circumstances to their purely psychological realities. Their perceptions create the symbols, and the reader witnesses what they see in their heightened emotional states. In such episodes, the physical world loses its matter-of-factness and the forms and relations occurring in it become schemata indicating psychic events. The correlation between the natural scene and individual subjectivity is the dominant and thematic metaphor of the fiction, and it is chiefly from this equation that Lawrence finds support for his tone of firm hopefulness. Ursula's history completes the novel's equation between Nature and the human unconscious, the "greater will" that Lawrence wished to liberate from the restrictions of society and mental consciousness. The continuous metaphor provides the moral standard by which actions are shown to be as blameless, life-giving and inevitable as nature itself— or as perverse, deadening, and needless as a desecration of nature.

But nothing in the novel explains why only the female characters maintain their identification with unconscious Nature, while the males abruptly lose their sensual power after the first generation of Brangwens. Tom Brangwen is the only man who is equal in sensual vitality to the woman he loves, and he is also the only male character whose experience and feelings are interesting to Lawrence and memorable to the reader. In the second generation, young Will Brangwen is introduced as a lover for Anna: he enters the novel on a contingency basis, and Lawrence allows him to remain a nondescript figure, interesting in the long run only because he *never* achieves fullness of character. After Tom, the men are not developed in the fiction. They are prejudged and presented by Lawrence as sensually incapacitated creatures, while the women in the Brangwensaga learn to thrive independently of their men. Lawrence purports to blame the male character's sensual failure on the sterility and degradation of contemporary culture, even though the heroic Ursula is fully exposed to every corrupting influence of modernity and yet she preserves her natural will to be herself. But Lawrence felt at a loss to explain the causes of sensual breakdown except by pointing to its effects in the mechanicalness of industrial civilization. His hope for a better future between men and women required him to replace present conditions, "the brittle corruption of houses and factories," with a whole new social order that would reflect the fulfillment of natural, individual character. Ursula's vision of the future projects a new civilization that will take its proper place in the continuity of nature. When Lawrence was asked to clarify the "message" of The Rainbow, he could answer only with an apocalyptic pronouncement: "I don't know myself what it is: except that the older world is done for, toppling on top of us: and that it's no use the men looking to the women for salvation, nor the women looking to sensuous satisfaction for their fulfillment. There must be a new world." (CL 422)

He believed, in 1915, that his novel might help initiate a growth of self-realization in mankind that would be comparable to the voyages in which the true geography of the world itself was first discovered. "I am correcting the proofs of the Rainbow," he wrote to Ottoline Morrel. "Whatever else it is, it is a voyage of discovery towards the real and eternal and unknown land. We are like Columbus, we have our backs upon Europe, till we come to the new world." (LH 244) This seemingly casual analogy between a new world of subjective fulfillment and the discovery of America is an early sign of the elaborate imaginative process by which Lawrence eventually made the actual, geographical New World into a symbolic place. By equating Nature with unconscious character he had already done much in *The Rainbow* to make the whole earth into a symbol of the features of the soul, and for the rest of his life Lawrence explored that symbolic material, continent by continent, in his art and in his travels. The central location for his symbolic projections came to be the American Southwest and Mexico. The region's primitive locales and the vastness of its uninhabited landscapes offered him new images of physical nature with which to define essential human nature. In discovering the startling Rocky Mountain region particularly, Lawrence refined and altered his vision of the natural and unconscious character of man.

But in 1915 his interest in America as a new world encouraging his personal hopes for a freer, more vital life had mainly a practical relevance to his immediate circumstances. Britain's intensifying war effort and the frustration of Lawrence's hope to reorganize society made him simply weary of life in England by the end of the summer. The United States, still an emphatically neutral country appeared to be a refuge from the atmosphere of war. Also, Lawrence's interest in a utopian colony revived when for a while he expected Frederick Delius to offer his abandoned Florida plantation as a site for Lawrence's Rananim. When that possibility waned, Lawrence inquired about other sites in Florida, and he applied for passports to America—with some justified worry that Frieda's German birth might restrict their freedom to leave the country. In October, in a letter to Harriet Monroe, the editor of *Poetry*, he wrote with grim enthusiasm about his plan to travel:

> I must see America: here the autumn of all life has set in, the fall: we are hardly more than the ghosts in the haze, we who stand apart from the flux of death. I must

see America. I think one can feel hope there. I think that
there the life comes up from the roots, crude but vital.
Here the whole tree of life is dying. It is like being
dead: the underworld. I must see America. I believe it is
beginning, not ending. (*LH* 266–67)

Lawrence very probably would have come to the United
States at that time, except for the postponement arising from
Scotland Yard's seizure on November 3 of the recently published *Rainbow*. The novel was suppressed and the action upheld by a police court, which fined the abject publisher,
Methuen, and ordered the remaining bound and unbound
copies to be destroyed. Lawrence at his first notification of
the seizure seemed too dispirited about the English public and
its government to make any defense of his work. But when it
appeared that other literary figures and some political persons
might unite to clear the novel from the charges of obscenity,
Lawrence reluctantly cancelled his plans to sail for New York
on November 24 and remained in London to participate in a
proposed legal battle that never materialized.[7]

The calumny against Lawrence in most of the press and the
temporary refusal of both publishers and printers to handle
any more major work by him ruined all of his opportunities
to gain a wide audience in England for several years to come.
The caution of the publishing industry also handicapped
other writers whose work might be construed as a political or
moral criticism of the present state of society, and the mood
of literary suppression was partly responsible for ending the
vitality of London literary life after its splendid flourishing
from 1911 to 1915. Ezra Pound found his own publisher in
London demanding unreasonable deletions from his poetry in
May 1916, and Pound ascribed the continuing general censorship to the notoriety of the *Rainbow* case. To Pound it

appeared—ironically enough, considering his earlier opinions—that America was the only place where one could at the moment find freedom for expression.[8] But in America shortly thereafter, government censorship suppressed *The Little Review* for publishing excerpts from Joyce's forthcoming *Ulysses*, and the *Review*'s editors were convicted of printing obscenity. Not suppressed as badly as Joyce—whose works were banned for twenty years in one or another English-speaking country, and in all three of them for about ten of those years—Lawrence was for a time cut off from the general public; no publisher in England or America dared touch the manuscript of *Women in Love* for four years after it was completed, until the novel was successfully launched by a private printing in New York in 1920.[9]

Thwarted, dejected, ill with another bronchial inflammation, and with hardly any money to spend or expect, Lawrence at the end of 1915—a year he later remembered as marking the end of everything creative in Western civilization—accepted the use of an empty house in Cornwall; and he and Frieda lived on that bleak coast for nearly two years. For a while Murry and Katherine Mansfield came to live in an adjacent cottage, and the four made an effort to abide by their mutual devotion in spite of all the distress within their individual lives and the antagonisms that broke out among them. The Lawrences were eventually compelled to leave Cornwall by local military authorities who suspected them of spying; they returned to London, because they were forbidden to live in any restricted security area; and even in London Scotland Yard maintained surveillance over the Lawrences until the end of the war. The stridency and bitterness of Lawrence's later accounts of these years' experiences must always be read with the recollection that only a few months before the frustrations began, Lawrence was brimful with his happy plans to reach "the best part, the believing part, the passionate, generous part" of the English soul and to teach it how to "go naked with its fellows." The shock of total, enforced alienation from a public that condemned him reverberates in his chapter on "The Nightmare" in *Kangaroo* and in his denunciation of war in his Introduction to *Memoirs of the Foreign Legion*.[10] The hyperbolic and defensive egotism of those passages records the extreme self-assertiveness that helped Lawrence weather his sudden and severe wartime isolation.

Lawrence intensified his criticism of present civilization in *Women in Love*, which he wrote while living in Cornwall. In this fiction he analyzes culture from a viewpoint that is more sociological and descriptive than the earlier book's historical perspective. "It is a novel which took its final shape in the midst of the period of war, though it does not concern the war itself," Lawrence stated in his Foreword. "I should wish the time to remain unfixed, so that the bitterness of the war may be taken for granted in the characters." *Women in Love* examines the unconscious roots of bitterness more analytically than *The Rainbow*, for in contrast to the preceding saga of Brangwen life, *Women in Love* treats experience that is individual rather than familial. The new novel, which Lawrence spoke of as "a kind of sequel to *The Rainbow*," continues to relate Ursula's story as she and her sister Gudrun meet their destined lovers, Rupert Birkin and Gerald Crich, contrasting types of men who become intimate friends. The corruption and doom that the novel finds chiefly in the love between Gerald and Gudrun are projected onto contemporary mankind as well. The narrative structure helps generalize Lawrence's judgment about the lovers' personal malaise, for as the characters move casually through the novel's five principal settings each location is shown to be a center of current, decadent civilization, as H. M. Daleski points out.[11]

Also generalizing Lawrence's apocalyptic outlook is the simple device of including various nationalities in the fiction. *Women in Love* has a heterogeneous cast of characters that nearly equals the universality and contrivance of *Moby-Dick*. The social classes are all represented, from sordid working-class lovers up to the titled nobility of England and the Continent, though the most prominent characters are middle-class and semi-professional people and bohemian artists. The mixture of personal types and origins blends realistically in the novel's social focus that is chiefly the sophisticated world of "advanced" and "emancipated" personalities. A Jew, a Russian, an Arab servant, an Italian countess, a British baronet, a Fraulein, a French governess, a German sculptor—each minor figure contributes some detail to the atmosphere of universal depravity and psychological dissolution that pervades the fiction. The numerous references to other cultures also generalize the theme, for they carry overtones of the destruction that came to earlier societies at a peak of their development. During an outburst of fury by his former mistress, Birkin is smashed over the head with a paperweight while he sits reading Thucydides' account of the fall of Athens. Birkin repeatedly recalls the fate of Sodom when he reflects on the decadence of contemporary people. The Italian countess reads Turgenev's analysis of moral anarchism in nineteenth-century Russia in *Fathers and Sons*. With detail upon detail Lawrence reinforces his statement that civilizations compound and express the force of corruption within individual lives.

The analysis of individual consciousness, however, is the principal intent of the novel, and the sense that grave troubles infect us is established in the first chapter—though many critics have noted that the opening scene disarmingly suggests a Jane Austen comedy about the reassertion of good hearts and civil manners. Ursula and Gudrun, sitting in the window-bay of their parents' substantial house in Beldover, where Ursula recuperated at the end of *The Rainbow*, discuss love and the prospect of marriage; and like vain or superior young ladies in fiction of more than a century earlier they are afraid that all married men are bores and that married life will not sustain the sense of heightened significance, the romantic vividness, that they require in life. Ursula complains that marriage is more than likely to be "the end of experience," and Gudrun extends this despondent observation with a comment about the dreariness of even their present lives: "Don't you find, that things fail to materialize? *Nothing materializes!* Everything withers in the bud." It is true, just as one expects from this sketch of the opening, that both women meet men who rouse their profoundest love and that the true nature and desires of each character do materialize. But within this narrative development the tone of presentation is ominous, not expectant. The *bud*, in Gudrun's reference to life in general, blossoms into a *fleur du mal* or a "flower of dissolution," which is Lawrence's phrase for the corrupt soul; and the essential natures of most of the characters are so badly disfigured psychologically that catastrophe and death fulfill their hearts' real desires.

The cause of their misery is, as always in Lawrence's view, a sensual failure, a breakdown of the human will to live an individual life. Throughout *Women in Love*, Lawrence and his spokesman, Birkin, try to promulgate a new set of values to recover the will and the means to natural fulfillment. Birkin preaches the viability of conjugal love as a foundation for all other human values, and every effort is made in the novel to convince us that the center of man's experience must be, as Birkin tells Gerald, a "perfect union with a woman—sort of ultimate marriage—and there isn't anything else." Such a marriage would reach deeper into character than a relationship of conscious love, Birkin believes, and it alone can revive the "stark, unknown beings" that people fundamentally are. "What I want is a strange conjunction with you," he explains to Ursula in a confession of love that disappoints her expectations of more romantic language; "not meeting and mingling . . . —but an equilibrium, a pure balance of two single beings:—as the stars balance each other." (XIII)

Birkin disavows the love-ideals that mask the violation of selves through "meeting and mingling," and "merging," and the clichéd patterns of being "in love." The principle of "balance" or *polarity* in love is fundamental to sensual vitality, he ✕ believes, for it preserves the inner, individual self intact. Though marriage offers the only opportunity for profound self-fulfillment, it paradoxically makes the severest attack upon one's separate identity. As an aid to maintaining "equilibrium," Birkin recommends another bond outside of marriage: an "eternal union with a man too: another kind of love." He looks to manly love as a necessary support to marriage and as a liberating extension of our unconscious life into a revivified civilization. Birkin achieves his "ultimate marriage" with Ursula, but lacking any enduring connection with another man he remains haunted by doom. At the end of the novel, as he sits over the body of Gerald who allowed himself to freeze to death in the mountains, Birkin feels devastated by the failure of their *Blutbruderschaft*, which would have given his friend strength to live if Gerald had held true to it. Weeping, he denounces the futile outcome of their friendship, and to the skeptical Ursula he insists that Gerald's acceptance of his offered love would have made a difference to them all. Birkin worries that neither mankind's self-destruction nor his own nagging "process of dissolution" can be arrested by the love in marriage only. But Ursula maintains a critical attitude in the concluding dialogue, and she condemns his interest in manly love as "an obstinacy, a theory, a perversity."

The end of the novel is filled with the air of tragic sorrow in Birkin's response to Gerald's death. His bitter lament indirectly eulogizes Gerald as the representative modern man, as he appears to most readers and critics—the ablest, fairest member of a society in which all men are doomed by their common limitation. Birkin's bitterness and grief alternate with his desperate conjecture that the total destruction of man is not truly a reason for despair. He tries to console himself with his old opinion that man is expendable in the universe, and that a humanless world will "carry on the embodiment of creation" after mankind plunges into oblivion. But his recurring pronouncements upon man's insignificance are seen throughout the fiction as the misanthropy of self-loathing which afflicts him. At one point, Ursula mocks him for trying to believe "simply in the end of the world, and in grass." In his self-renewal through love for her, Birkin casts off his "sham spirituality," his "death-eating," that Ursula excoriates in their lovers' quarrel. (XIII) The reappearance of his outworn viewpoint emphasizes Birkin's pathetic sense of futility over Gerald's momentous death. *Women in Love* concludes with the dramatization of an irrevocable loss that is both personal and universal, for the whole of the novel mourns the imminent end of *man*, and no sophistry about life continuing without him remains equal to the emotion that is sustained in the last chapter.

W. W. Robson finds that in the tragic tone of the conclusion the tale asserts its own moral: that the kind of love which Birkin sought has proved illusory.[12] But the novel fully dramatizes the triumph of his love with Ursula, a triumph of sensual will that has enabled them to break all their connections with society and with apparent success to "wander away from the world's somewhere, into our own nowhere." (XXIII) The bitter defeat in Birkin's history is the failure of his ideal of manly love, which threatens to undermine all love and marriage. His desire for an "eternal union" with Gerald is not merely a stubborn theory, as Ursula dismisses it, nor is the theme separable from the novel's investigation of love between men and women. The friendship between Birkin and Gerald unifies the otherwise divided structure of the novel, for the romances of the two couples have one central source and development in their analysis of homoerotic desire. Gerald's suicide has an air of tragedy because the emotional focus of the book as a whole, including the interest of the author and the sequence of narrative events, makes Gerald seem the most admired sexual figure and the dominant erotic presence in the fiction. When his death shows that love between men is probably impossible, both Birkin and Lawrence respond with a grief far more desperate and moving than their sorrow over woman's love. The heartbreak over Gerald is unmatched in Lawrence's work except at the conclusion of *Sons and Lovers* when Lawrence suffers with Paul over the death of Mrs. Morel. The comparable intensity of feeling in these situations suggests their connection in the soul of the author, where all the fictional characters and events reveal Lawrence's unconscious. Birkin's quest for homoerotic love is a consequence of Paul's romance with his mother, and both experiences lead to the defeat of a forbidden, covert, supreme desire.

The differences in subject and argument between the two works show how many complexities Lawrence was discovering in his experience of foredoomed love.

Lawrence was probably pursuing an actual homosexual romance in one or more of his friendships while writing *Women in Love*. Frieda refers vaguely to such a period in his life, and in *Kangaroo* Lawrence recounts the misery of such a relationship during his Cornwall years specifically.[13] But quite apart from this biographical suggestion, it is evident from a rejected Prologue to *Women in Love* that Lawrence at this time strongly felt that homoeroticism was the chief complication in all sexual experience. In the unpublished first chapter Lawrence gives a full report of Birkin's tormented homosexual desires and an account of the mutual erotic attraction between him and Gerald. The opening paragraphs recount their initial meeting in the Tyrol four years earlier, when each man instantly "knew the trembling nearness" of the other, and though they maintain reserve and neither one acknowledges it: "they knew they loved each other, that each would die for the other." During the four years before they meet again at the beginning of the novel's narrative action, Birkin suffers from his sexual ambivalence which he cannot accept morally. His desires, nevertheless, are fully conscious: men rouse his sexual passion, and he longs to possess the bodies of nameless strangers. He is intoxicated by the sexual beauty of two types of men:

> White-skinned, keen limbed men with eyes like blue-flashing ice and hair like crystals of winter sunshine, the northmen, inhuman as sharp-crying gulls, distinct like splinters of ice, like crystals, isolated, individual; and then the men with dark eyes that one can enter and plunge into, bathe in, as in a liquid darkness, dark-

skinned, supple, night-smelling men, who are the living substance of the viscous, universal heavy darkness. (P2 105)

In this report of Birkin's homoerotic feelings, one immediately recognizes the sensations and the very words that in the novel are not Birkin's but Gudrun's responses to Gerald and to Loerke, who typify the two classes of sexually attractive men. Lawrence transferred to her the feelings that would have been Birkin's if his homosexuality had become explicitly the central issue in the fiction. Her distorted feelings of love— her pursuit of pain in sexual contact with brutal, relentless force—has no other origin or consonance in the novel. Gudrun is physically and mentally glamorous, full of young beauty, strength, awareness, and pride. Yet she is damned to pursue extreme psychological and sexual sensations in which she anticipates her doom. The paradox—plausible as it could be among the complexities of an actual life—is never made comprehensible in the fiction. The only explanation for her character is that Lawrence chose to make her the vehicle of feelings that he originally understood to be homoerotic, and that her responses give evidence of Lawrence's shame and anxiety over such desires.

It is possible that Lawrence was trying to minimize or disguise his views about homosexuality, especially since the suppression of *The Rainbow* had just shown him that the treatment of sex in fiction could not be freely outspoken. Birkin's latent homosexuality remains prominent through implication even without the Prologue to clarify his psychology, and Gerald's troubled sexual response to Birkin appears clearly in the episodes that dramatize his resistance to their *Blutbruderschaft*. But the important effect of transferring Birkin's sensations onto Gudrun is that the change generalizes Lawrence's

views. He shifts the atmosphere of perversion on to heterosexual relations, alleging them to be hopelessly complicated by
homosexual ambivalence. Gerald and Gudrun anticipate the
fulfillment of their romance in an aura of revulsion, hysteria,
and disaster. The sado-masochism of their affair is fully described, but its causes remain half hidden in Lawrence's
implication that both Gerald and Gudrun—even more than
Birkin—need "another kind of love."

In the opening chapter Gudrun instantly recognizes that
Gerald is her destined lover, because of his air of invulnerable
sexual mastery. She thrills with anticipation of some extreme
conflict between them, and throughout the first half of the
novel she reels with excitement at every meeting with Gerald.
Her passion exalts her fear of violence in masculine sexuality,
which she hopes to master by her attitude of exquisite subjection. Gerald's response to her, however, develops much
slower and more deviously; his attraction to Gudrun is not a
direct response to her but a displacement of feelings roused in
him by other circumstances.

The doom that pervades Gerald's life is not his fear of
heterosexual love but his rejection of love between men. His
"process of dissolution" that ends in suicide begins with his
accidental killing of his brother, for that act comes to symbolize his denial of any life-tie among men. He is fundamentally a "murderer," as Lawrence warns us in the second chapter, and all of his energies serve to destroy life for him and for
others. After his definitive childhood "accident" Gerald pursues his own death through violent masculine exploits as a
soldier, explorer, and sportsman. He is repeatedly placed
amidst water and snow as a swimmer or skier, and the cold,
aqueous substances which are his special element in the novel
consistently suggest Gerald's attraction to death. In his social

role, Gerald projects his own despair of life onto a whole class of society. As a leading industrialist, he modernizes the coal-mining industry and settles the series of strikes and labor riots at the Crich family's mines. With intuitive sympathy for the miners' sense of degradation by technological changes, Gerald leads the workers to revere mechanical productiveness itself because he senses that worship of the machine exalts their inhuman, repetitive actions. After a period of violent resistance to modernization, the men—like Gerald's mistress—find a perverse satisfaction in abandoning themselves to his power. The mining operation as reorganized by Gerald into an efficient industry expresses the common man's despair and rejection of spontaneous, warm life.

In Birkin as in others, Gerald rouses an anticipation of new knowledge and new activity. Gerald desires but hesitates to accept the attachment of manly love that Birkin would freely welcome as an adjunct to marriage. Birkin recognizes that Gerald's resistance is upheld by a defining, fixed principle of his character that prevents any widening of his experience:

> This strange sense of fatality in Gerald, as if he were limited to one form of existence, one knowledge, one activity, a sort of fatal halfness, which to himself seemed wholeness, always overcame Birkin after their moments of passionate approach, and filled him with a sort of contempt, or boredom. It was the insistence on the limitation which so bored Birkin in Gerald. (XVI)

After Birkin's illness occasions a crisis of erotic feelings in their friendship, Gerald finds himself bored with all his usual satisfactions—work, sexual adventures, hashish, or travel. He recovers new spirit only when Birkin visits him one night and the two men abandon themselves to frenzied physical contact by wrestling. Birkin tries to explain to him that their intimacy and physical attraction are perfectly wholesome: " 'We are mentally, spiritually intimate, therefore we should be more or less physically intimate too—it is more whole.' " Though Gerald agrees to Birkin's happy rational conclusion, he remains troubled and confused by the power of his feeling for a man. At the end of the chapter, "Gladitorial," Gerald haltingly confesses that he does not expect love for a woman to equal his genuine love for Birkin. After "a long pause," Birkin answers cautiously and vaguely in an effort to encourage his friend: " 'Life has all kinds of things,' said Birkin. 'There isn't only one road.' " But the desperate tone of Gerald's response indicates his distress over pursuing any other than the usual satisfactions. Frightened by the appeal of a "bloodbrotherhood," he can conceive of his fulfillment only as ominous and final:

> "Yes, I believe that too. I believe it. And mind you, I don't care how it is with me—I don't care how it is—so long as I don't feel—" he paused, and a blank, barren look passed over his face, to express his feeling—"so long as I feel I've *lived*, somehow—and I don't care how it is—but I want to feel that—" (XX)

Precisely at this halfway point in the narrative, Gerald's casual attraction to Gudrun turns into a consuming passion that supersedes any further development of love between him and Birkin. Gerald surprises himself and astonishes the elated Gudrun by declaring his love for her. Gudrun, who looks on Gerald with rapacious expectation of sinister pleasures, captures all the force of Gerald's conflicting needs. She offers to satisfy his pent-up desire for a sexual experience that transgresses his psychological limits, and she also preserves his belief in his glamorous masculinity. Gudrun holds Gerald entranced with desire for a woman, while he experiences with her the "licentiousness"—the sexual extremism and barbaric feelings—that would characterize his guilt-ridden participation in a homosexual act. He turns to her in a passion of flight from the alternative that Birkin's love presents.

The circumstances of Gerald's first sexual intercourse with Gudrun illustrate that his desire for her signifies his psychological disintegration. The chapter "Death and Love" deals chiefly with Gerald's misery at home during the last days of the elder Crich, who as a macabre and pathetic death's-head figure has dominated the entire household throughout his long illness. In theme and feeling, the chapter centers in the unendurable strain of a protracted crisis, which Lawrence establishes in the opening sentences: "Thomas Crich died slowly, terribly slowly. It seemed impossible to everybody that the thread of life could be drawn out so thin, and yet not break." Thomas Crich's personal *will*—the fixed, rational purposiveness of his character—finally crumbles, and the death of the elder Crich illustrates the defeat of the principle by which Gerald attempts to dominate life. The fatal limitation that Birkin recognized in him has visibly broken down; but with full understanding of the tragedy in the psychological event, Lawrence shows that the breakdown of an evil principle in Gerald is an emotional degeneration, not a psychic triumph for him. In deep suffering, Gerald visits his father's fresh grave on a rainy night, and then desperately plunges toward the Brangwen house, where surreptitiously and dripping with clay he enters Gudrun's bedroom. Mutely demanding sexual consummation, Gerald empties himself of anxieties during a love-scene that is dominated by images of his infantile dependency. His turning to Gudrun in this context signifies a regressive response to the crisis of "invisible physical life" brought on by his father's dying. Unnerved, he settles himself through sexual exhaustion with Gudrun, and "he found in her an infinite relief."

The death of Thomas Crich occurs when Gerald is at a peak of disturbed vacillation over Birkin's love. The narrative structure coalesces Gerald's responses to these parallel mysteries of love and death, and in one definitive action Gerald evades both his crises. His reaction is a narcissistic exploitation of Gudrun: "Like a child at the breast, he cleaved intensely to her, and she could not put him away." Broken by the knowledge of death and by a sexual ambivalence that he cannot accept, Gerald's soul falls into a "process of dissolution." In the remaining months of his life he pursues the sensation of self-destruction in his affair with Gudrun, demanding specifically the explosive force of tortured orgasm, while Gudrun easily dominates him by offering herself only to his frenzies of abuse. He explains to Birkin that Gudrun is his supreme experience, and his expression reveals that in loving Gudrun he seeks only the final obliteration of consciousness:

> "There's something final about this. And Gudrun seems like the end, to me. I don't know—but she seems so soft, her skin like silk, her arms heavy and soft. And it withers my consciousness, somehow, it burns the pith of my mind." He went on a few paces, staring ahead, his eyes fixed, looking like a mask used in ghastly religions of the barbarians. "It blasts your soul's eye," he said, "and leaves you sightless. Yet you *want* to be sightless, you *want* to be blasted, you don't want it any different."
> He was speaking as if in a trance, verbal and blank. Then suddenly he braced himself up with a kind of rhapsody, and looked at Birkin with vindictive, cowed eyes, saying:
> "Do you know what it is to suffer when you are with a woman? She's so beautiful, so perfect, you find her *so*

good, it tears you like a silk, and every stroke and bit cuts hot—ha, that perfection, when you blast yourself, you blast yourself! And then—" he stopped on the snow and suddenly opened his clenched hands—"it's nothing —your brain might have gone charred as rags—and—" he looked round into the air with a queer histrionic movement—"it's blasting—you understand what I mean —it is a great experience, something final—and then— you're shrivelled as if struck by electricity." He walked on in silence. It seemed like bragging, but like a man in extremity bragging truthfully.

"Of course," he resumed, "I wouldn't *not* have had it! It's a complete experience. And she's a wonderful woman. But—how I hate her somewhere! It's curi- ous—"

Birkin looked at him, at his strange, scarcely con- scious face. Gerald seemed blank before his own words.

"But you've had enough now?" said Birkin. "You have had your experience. Why work on an old wound?"

"Oh," said Gerald, "I don't know. It's not finished—" (XXIX)

The finish occurs when Gerald in an unendurable rage against Gudrun is overcome by nausea and revulsion for all of life. He drops her in the snow, half-strangled, and he turns away to meet his death by freezing on the mountain peaks. The catastrophe takes place amidst the symbolic landscape of the Tyrol, where Lawrence in the Prologue had originally be- gun the romance between Gerald and Birkin. The extended description of the place itself is one of Lawrence's finest achievements in the novel, for the crystalline and massive landscape, which is breathtakingly vivid, comes to be emo- tionally abhorrent as it reveals its symbolic meaning. The Al- pine setting is the culmination of Lawrence's identifications between Gerald's condition of rigidly limited consciousness and all *cold* substances. The mountain is also the geographical image of the "slope of death" which Birkin has pictured as the present footing of the northern European soul in its last stage of dissolution. The kinesthetic force of the landscape mirrors the crushing antagonism that lies scarcely below the surface of heterosexual love between Gerald and Gudrun. In the sequence of composition that reveals Lawrence's discoveries and developing judgments about his subject, the place of budding love between man and man becomes the final setting that commemorates like a tombstone man's demented will to crush the life out of himself. In this, as in every way, the novel implies that the bitterness of the heterosexual affair and Gerald's tragic death are the consequences of man's fear to love his friend.

The story of Birkin, who is the central figure in the novel, is intended to illustrate the triumph of the psychically liberated man who learns to acknowledge his homoerotic feelings and to value them as part of his full, spontaneous sensual nature. Birkin's moods of despair and petulance early in the narrative are signs of a crippled emotional state, in which for years he has prolonged an ambiguous affair with Hermione. Even without the Prologue's explanation one sees that Birkin's life is complicated by a fear of women and a sensual attraction to men. Roused to new love in his relationship with Ursula, he slowly manages to erase his image of her as a Magna Mater full of Woman's greed to possess and dismember her sexual victim. Birkin's progress toward a sane response to Ursula is measured chiefly by their extended discussions about love and by their mercurial quarrels that displace his fears and allow the lovers to express trust and tenderness. But along with this love story, the narrative traces the simultaneous growth of Birkin's attraction to Gerald. Birkin more ardently and openly seeks Gerald's love as his romance with Ursula proves successful and vivifying for him. Lawrence hoped to show through Birkin that the free, unified man will express his sensual affections, his unconscious feelings, in every relationship with things and persons—not just with the opposite sex. Lawrence relieved Birkin of the guilty feelings that in the Prologue complicated his desires in order to make him into a test-case of the exemplary, "new world" man. When Gerald perversely dies, however, neither Birkin nor Lawrence can overcome the feeling that the ideal of manly love has resulted in catastrophe—and the novel concludes with this misgiving and lament.

The failure of the homoerotic ideal in *Women in Love* left Lawrence's ambivalence toward women more acute than before. Disposed to identify with his female characters as the vessels of sensual life in *Sons and Lovers* and *The Rainbow*, he was at the same time hypersensitive to any distortions of masculine identity, and he held women responsible for the possessive love that warps an individual's natural integrity. In *Women in Love* Lawrence more analytically explores the ambiguities that account for love's strange facts. His characterization of Birkin shows that Birkin's image of the devouring female expresses, in part, his fascinated dread of being assaulted as a female by a dismembering, "murdering" male. In his corrective effort to love both woman and man, Birkin's homosexual fantasy very nearly comes true. He is not assaulted by Gerald, but it seems that Gerald averts that fate only because he is psychologically constrained to destroy himself rather than murder or "blast" his friend. Lawrence's own anxiety over the male eros, which sets the tragic tone of the catastrophe, leads him to undermine his analysis throughout the book by dramatizing the fantasy explanation that woman destroys all manliness. This charge against the devouring female, though disproved by Ursula, is laid against Gudrun, whose genesis as Birkin's persona remains evident in the novel. Birkin's failure to heal himself reinforces the emotional truth of Gudrun the man-as-woman, the sexually defensive destroyer of natural life. The novel is true to the author's feelings, but it betrayingly confirms his fears; and consequently, this novel is followed by Lawrence's increasingly hostile representations of women through his subsequent works, until he desperately extricated himself from active sexuality altogether.

But in *Women in Love* the failure of love to prove fully therapeutic is softened by the vague surmise that love between men and women cannot be entirely futile, however solitary and doomed the heroic lovers appear when all the richly symbolic facts of the novel suggest their isolation and defeat. Birkin and Ursula, having brought their sensual selves into flower, find themselves alienated from all of contemporary European life, with nothing to do that will not violate their integrity and no place to live that will not overwhelm them with humanity's smell of death. They detach themselves from each of the novel's principal settings; they give up their jobs, they give up their homes, and by the end of the novel they have become wanderers headed toward sunny Mediterranean lands. To Gudrun, who cautions that "the only thing to do with the world is to see it through," Ursula replies that "One has no more connections here. One has a sort of other self, that belongs to a new planet, not to this. You've got to hop off." (XXIX) She and Birkin are set to voyage beyond the novel's horizons to find a place where daily life will directly fulfill man's deepest nature. Surely for Birkin this destined place must allow the freest expression of love between man and man, and Lawrence directs him toward the Mediterranean as a region where one is likely to find the spontaneous expression of masculine affections.

Lawrence himself longed to return to a warmer, sunnier climate, because of his chronic bronchial inflammations. He thought of returning to Italy, and the possibility of going to Florida lingered in his imagination. He needed to escape the damp cold of northern Europe; but, believing what he wrote about the European soul, he also needed to begin his search for a more perfect arena of the soul's unconscious life. *Women in Love* articulates the beliefs and feelings at the very center of his character; and the novel establishes, in theme and tone and imagery, all Lawrence's requirements for the new world civilization that he subsequently pursued around four continents through years of travel and writing. Analyzing false leads and frail promises in Italy, Sicily, Sardinia, Ceylon, and Australia, his imagination repeatedly turned back to one lasting possibility of renewal for mankind: only America offered a history, a literature, and a landscape that amplified Lawrence's profoundest vision in *Women in Love*.

4

"To transfer all my life to America"

While *The Rainbow* remained suppressed and the manuscript of *Women in Love* was being refused by London publishers, Lawrence saw that a more responsive audience awaited him in the United States. During the destitute period in Cornwall he was partly supported by gifts of money from Americans, and American magazines were paying him as much for three or four poems as an entire volume of verse earned him in England. He began to consider the United States not just as a possible site for Rananim but as his proper public: "I believe that England . . . is capable of not seeing anything but badness in me, for ever and ever. I believe America is my virgin soil, truly." (*CL* 494) He asked Cynthia Asquith to help him plead his financial hardship to obtain renewed passports to the United States: "I am pretty sure of selling my stuff if I am in America. . . . It is quite useless my trying to live and write here. I shall only starve in ignominy: should be starving now if an American hadn't given me £60." (*CL* 496) At the same time, he urged Catherine Carswell, who was having difficulty in bringing forth a novel: "*Write for America* if you can't write. I find I am unable to write for England any more—the response has gone quite dead and dumb. A certain hope rises in my heart, quite hot, and I can go on. But it is not England. It seems to me it is America. If I am kept here I am beaten for ever." (*CL* 498)

The exhortation to Mrs. Carswell indicates that economic advantage remained only part of America's inducement as a land of hope for Lawrence. During these scarcely hopeful years his letters show that any chance connection with American life was apt to rouse a renewed desire in him to travel to the new world and initiate another era:

> We have had here two Americans. Americans are as a rule rather dreadful, I think. They are *not* younger than we, but older: a second childhood. But being so old, in senile decay and second childishness, perhaps they are nearer to the end, and the new beginning.
> I *know* now, finally:
> (a) That I want to go away from England for ever.
> (b) That I want *ultimately* to go to a country of which I have hope, in which I feel the new unknown.
> In short, I want, immediately or at length, to transfer all my life to America. Because there, I know, the *skies* are not so old, the air is newer, the earth is not tired. Don't think I have any illusions about the people, the life. The people and the life are monstrous. I want, at length, to get a place in the far west mountains, from which one can see the distant Pacific Ocean, and there live facing the bright west. But I also think that America, being so much *worse*, falser, further gone than England, is nearer to freedom. England has a long and awful process of corruption and death to go through. America has dry-rotted to a point where the final *seed* of the new is almost left ready to sprout. When I can, I shall go to America, and find a place. (*CL* 481–82)

Underlying his conviction, there was, as usual, a new piece of work taking shape and generating his zeal. Within a few weeks after finishing *Women in Love* Lawrence began a careful study of American literature, in which he formulates his conception of a symbolic America and its crucial role in the history of man's consciousness. In a series of essays which was later to become, in a greatly altered version, the *Studies in Classic American Literature*,[1] Lawrence examines the responses of eighteenth- and nineteenth-century writers to the spirit of place in the New World, and he finds that American literature and history substantiate his correlations between unconscious character, nature, and civilization. When he finished the study in the summer of 1918, he regarded it as the fruit not of eighteen months' work but of over four years of continuous preparation, for he believed that his viewpoint had been forming steadily through all his fiction and essays since 1914. He felt that he was extrapolating theories implicit in his earlier works and formulating them intellectually as a proof of his insights—a periodic procedure with him, that he was later to call wryly "pollyanalytics." He spoke of the essays as his "philosophy"—not his literary criticism—and he declared that "it is absolutely necessary to get it out, fix it, and have a definite foothold, to be *sure*." (CL 546) Especially during his virtual confinement in Cornwall and his alienation from the English public, he needed reassurance of the rational, systematic coherence of his artistic vision. Bitterly wary, however, he anticipated another rebuff from English readers; and after eight of the twelve essays were printed in the *English Review* from November 1918 to June 1919 the editors refused the rest. Anxious to keep the series together as an integral work, Lawrence offered it as a book written "for America."

He wrote worrisomely to B. W. Huebsch, his new American publisher:

> These essays are the result of five years of persistent work. They contain a whole *Weltanschauung*—new, if old—even a new science of psychology—pure science. I don't want to give them to a publisher here—not yet.—I don't really want people to read them—till they are in cold print. I don't mind if you don't publish them—or if you keep them back.—I only know the psychoanalysts here—one of them—has gone to Vienna, partly to graft some of the ideas on to Freud and the Freudian theory of the unconscious—is at this moment busy doing it. I *know* they are trying to get the theory of primal consciousness out of these essays, to solidify their windy theory of the unconscious. Then they'll pop out with it, as a discovery of their own.—You see I've told Ernest Jones and the Eders the ideas.—But they don't know how to use them. And no one has seen the essay on Whitman—no one in the world.—Look after the MS. for me, won't you.—Schaff says you're the only "white" publisher in America.—Superlative. (*CL* 595-96)

Lawrence was defensive and jealous and secretive in a way he had never been about his earlier work. The essays were precious to him because—among several reasons—they translate his intuitions made through art into the discursive language of rational thought. This distinction between "art-speech" and "plain speech" is one of the major points made by the essays: art speaks its truth in a symbolic language, Lawrence says, in which often "the intellectual idea remains implicit, latent and nascent." Art is man's most expressive language, because it issues from all levels of his experience and communicates a whole state of being—"emotional and pas-

sional, spiritual and perceptual, all at once." (*SM* 19) In the
highest art, both the emotional and intellectual levels adequately register the experience realized by the other; creative
passion and explicit idea balance each other in "pure art,
where the sensual mind is harmonious with the ideal mind."
(*SM* 136) But it happens in periods of great change in man's
experience that one kind of awareness advances far beyond
the other, and art speaks in a double voice that reveals the
split within man's consciousness.

The double voice is evident in modern literature generally,
in which an author's predominant ideal consciousness imposes
a strict moralism upon his sensual response to life. But the
double voice is particularly prominent in American writing,
for "American art-speech reveals what the American plain
speech almost deliberately conceals":

> What Hawthorne deliberately says in *The Scarlet Let-
> ter* is on the whole a falsification of what he uncon-
> sciously says in his art-language. And this, again, is one
> of the outstanding qualities of American literature: that
> the deliberate ideas of the man veil, conceal, obscure
> that which the artist has to reveal. This quality of du-
> plicity which runs through so much of the art of the
> modern world is almost inevitable in an American book.
> The author is unconscious of it himself. He is sincere in
> his own intention. And yet, all the time, the artist, who
> writes as a somnambulist, in the spell of pure truth as in
> a dream, is contravened and contradicted by the wake-
> ful man and moralist who sits at the desk. (*SM* 18)

Lawrence argues that the American writer unconsciously
expresses the profound sensuality of the new continent, the
spirit of the physical place itself, but his mind remains imprisoned by old ideas that were once relevant to another hemisphere in another era. Like the Latin writings of the Church

Fathers in Africa during the Roman decadence, American literature contains "the incipient realities of a whole new era of experience":

> It is the quality of life-experience, of emotion and passion and desire, which has changed in the Romans of Africa, and in the English-speaking Americans. Life itself takes on a new reality, a new motion, even while the idea remains ostensibly the same. (*SM* 17)

Throughout the essays Lawrence is deliberately concerned to show evidence of the corruption of European Christian consciousness, which is even more decadent—"further gone" —in America than in England. The theme of the study is that "American art symbolizes the destruction, decomposition, mechanizing of the fallen degrees of consciousness." (*SM* 235) Lawrence claims that American literature bears witness to a collapse of the quality of life which fulfilled European man from the early medieval period to the late Renaissance, and that the history of the white man in the western hemisphere records the modern European's final disintegration under the spell of his unconscious loathing of life. But listening to the old soul's extremity of death in "the sad, weird utterance of this classic America," one may still find signs of the next, new era of life "when the new world sets in":

> At present there is a vast myriad-branched human engine, the very thought of which is death. But in the winter even a tree looks like iron. Seeing the great trunk of dark iron and the swaying steel flails of boughs, we cannot help being afraid. What we see of buds looks like sharp bronze stud-points. The whole thing hums elastic and sinister and fatally metallic, like some confused scourge of swinging steel thongs. Yet the lovely cloud of green and summer lustre is within it. (*SM* 30)

Preliminary to his analysis of American books, Lawrence explains the "greater inhuman forces" that drew the emotionally decadent European to the wilderness of America in the first place. While the spirituality of medieval Europe was in a healthy condition, man's full nature was vigorously reflected by the polarity between the centers of civilization in spiritual Rome and sensual Germany. At that time, as similarly in every period of mature civilization, the two geographical poles served to affirm and oppose the dominant character of the times, and their balanced opposition offered expression for the complete range of human potentiality within the religious spirit of their era. But when the "great mystic passion of medieval life" weakened and the balance between sensual and spiritual consciousness was destroyed, life at the extremes of the "magnetic" circuit was drawn away by new fields of force. The European religious impulse was sundered at the Renaissance, and that part of its energy which was constrictive and repressive turned to exert itself against another center of sensual opposition.

From the opposite half of the earth the American continent with its fecund wilderness and red-colored savages sent disruptive meanings into the lives of restive Europeans. The place—"dark, violent, aboriginal"—stimulated new promptings of sensual awareness in them and attracted their unconscious will to gain power over the symbolic meaning of the continent. Myriads of colonizers and adventurers were drawn "like birds down the great electric direction of the west, lifted like migrating birds on a magnetic current." They went for reasons other than those they realized, going neither for wealth nor for religious liberty. Calvinists, Puritans, Spaniards of the Inquisition, flocked across the ocean to dominate and repress the new world's image of their abhorred sensual, spontaneous nature.

"The great field for the lust of control in the modern world is America," Lawrence says. The history of the discoverers and settlers of this country is "a disheartening, painful record of the lusting triumph of the deliberate will." Having come to conquer a wilderness, the first Americans firmly dominated their natural passions and managed to subject all life to the urgent requirements of purposive work. Productiveness became compulsive, a regulated, predictable behavior that destroyed the last vestiges of individual, passional life and the creative impulse:

> The New Englanders, wielding the sword of the spirit backwards, struck down the primal impulsive being in every man, leaving only a mechanical, automatic unit. In so doing they cut and destroyed the living bond between men, the rich passional contact. And for this passional contact gradually was substituted the mechanical bond of purposive utility. The spontaneous passion of social union once destroyed, then it was possible to establish the perfect mechanical concord, the concord of a number of parts to a vast whole, a stupendous productive mechanism. And this, this vast mechanical concord of innumerable machine-parts, each performing its own motion in the intricate complexity of material production, this is the clue to the western democracy. (*SM* 27)

The modern American, true to his heritage, functions with automatic concord in the mechanical complexity of industrial production and democratic society: "having conquered and destroyed the instinctive, impulsive being in himself, he is free to be always deliberate, always calculated, rapid, swift, and single in practical execution as a machine." (*SM* 28) The goal of American civilization is to perfect the institutions that eliminate all "passions, prides, impulses of the self which cause disparity between one human being and another"; and the record of American literature shows "the pattern or standard man" striving for mastery over his contrary self in the symbolic meaning of the wilderness, the Indian, the white whale, the witches of the flesh and forest, the oceans, and ultimately the cosmos itself. From Benjamin Franklin to Walt Whitman, Lawrence traces the changes in the American psyche that accompany "the process of forming a deliberate, self-conscious, self-determined humanity which, in the acceptance of a common idea of equality and fraternity, should be quite homogeneous, unified, ultimately dispassionate, rational, utilitarian." (*SM* 42)

Franklin appears to Lawrence as "the most admirable little automaton the world has ever seen," because he joyfully and systematically improved himself—"broke the impulses in himself," is Lawrence's phrase—by drawing up a list of virtues to practice until they became the habits of his behavior. He made himself over into an ideal being formed according to fixed precepts. In him, Lawrence says, the idea of the perfectibility of man was actually fulfilled, as nearly as possible, before that ideal galvanized Europe in the late eighteenth and early nineteenth centuries. All of Franklin's extraordinary energy went into fabricating a self for the efficient operation of daily affairs:

> It is a wonderful little snuff-coloured figure, so admirable, so *clever*, a little pathetic, and, somewhere, ridiculous and detestable.
>
> . . . He saw himself as a little unit in the vast total of society. All he wanted was to run well, as a perfect little wheel within the whole.
>
> The beauty of incomparable *being* was nothing to him. (*SM* 46)

Learning to live "entirely from his consciousness and his will," Franklin exemplifies the process of "inexorable repression" in America; but the deliberate reduction of life will lead, just as inevitably, to a rebirth of man whole and free:

> This process of attaining to unison by conquering and subduing all impulses, this removing of all those individual traits which make for separateness and diversity, had to be achieved and accomplished. It is not until man has utterly seized power over himself, and gained complete knowledge of himself, down to the most minute and shameful of his desires and sensations, that he can really begin to be free. Then, when man knows *all*, both shameful and good, that is in man; and when he has control over every impulse, both good and bad; then, and only then, having utterly bound and fettered himself in his own will and his own self-conscious knowledge, will he learn to make the great choice, the choice between automatic self-determining, and mystic, spontaneous freedom. (*SM* 48)

Franklin is the end product of Christian ethical development. His counterpart is Crèvecœur, the end product of Christian feeling: "They are the last instances of ethical England and emotional France, and together they make the complete American." (*SM* 54) In his *Letters from an American Farmer* Crèvecœur displays bits of immediate, sensual sympathy with insects, birds, and reptiles that enter his conventional description of idealized domestic life in a pastoral setting— complete with an "amiable spouse," their "healthy offspring," and red-skinned Children of Nature for neighbors. Crèvecœur could never see men in any terms but the roles prescribed by his humanitarian doctrines and romantic fancies; but looking at hornets or hummingbirds or the fight of two large snakes, he escapes from his sentimentality and responds to the actual, intrinsic being and otherness of unconscious creatures. Only the wilderness caught his deepest awareness and touched his sensual understanding:

He wanted, of course, to know the dark, savage way
of life, within the unlimited sensual impulse. He wanted
to know as the Indians and savages know, darkly, and in
terms of otherness. But this desire in him was very
strictly kept down by a fixed will. For he was absolutely
determined that Nature is sweet and pure, that all men
are brothers, and equal, and that they love one another
like so many cooing doves. He was determined to have
life according to his own prescription. Therefore, he
wisely kept away from any too close contact with Nature, and took refuge in commerce and the material
world. (*SM* 67)

As an unconscious artist, instead of a self-persuaded "emotional idealist," Crèvecœur recognized in wild life "the pride,
the recoil, the jewel-like isolation of the vivid self." (*SM* 61)
Though all of American life mitigates against this quality of
separateness and difference, the natural world blazons the
truth which Americans must eventually realize and honor:

The true self is like a star which must preserve the
circumambient darkness which gives to it its distinction
and uniqueness. It must keep the splendid, vivid loneliness. Dawn only removes the gulf from between the
stars, and makes them as nothing in the great one web of
light, the universal sun-consciousness, the selfless spiritual being. (*SM* 60)

Lawrence denounces American political democracy for re-
moving the gulf between men and subjecting all individuals to
the falsification of one mass identity. The fixed principle of
equality among men, whatever their nature, reduces humanity
to the same level as leaves of grass. The decadence of present
democracy and its terrible burden on the soul are shown
clearly, Lawrence observes, in Fenimore Cooper's Effingham
novels. The refined, genteel Effinghams are harassed by

Septimus Dodge of Dodgetown, who is a self-made man, like Benjamin Franklin, but is nothing more than a contemptible, importunate boor. Inwardly inferior and cringing, he claims his equality with the Effinghams, who have impaled their souls on their belief in the equality of men and in social liberty. Inwardly natural aristocrats, they writhe with pain but they hold true to their republican ideals.

Lawrence sees this overriding social assumption as a violation of natural life, another instance of the modern repression of unconscious, sensual vitality. But democracy in the future can presumably become organic and natural. It will not primarily make citizens, Lawrence says, but, instead, it will allow individuals to maintain their separate integrity and resist the pressures of merely social force:

> We must live in a world of perilous, pure freedom, having always the tincture of fear, danger, and exultance. Nothing else will keep us living. As jewels are crushed between the valves of the earth, and driven, through unutterable resistance, into their own clear perfection, leaving the matrix exempt; so must the human soul be purified in unspeakable resistance to the mass. We wear the ruby and the sapphire as symbols of our splendid pride in singleness, our jewel-like self. (*SM* 87)

Lawrence's concept of true democracy is a social extension of the *Blutbruderschaft* that Birkin sought with Gerald. Organic democracy is founded not on a concept of the masses but, instead, on a direct, sensual communion of respect and empathy among unique souls. In social relationships, this love finds expression in yielding authority to the superior vitality of a leader among men, and the hierarchy that results is not subjection or mastery, Lawrence says, but the natural culmination of self in sympathy with a greater self. In American literature the roots of this democracy of the future appear in the relations between white heroes and their savage companions. Cooper's Leatherstocking novels celebrate the perfect relationship of Natty and Chingachgook; between them there is a delicate, unsophisticated *Blutbruderschaft:*

> That which Chingachgook was, Natty was not; nor could he ever know. In the same way, Natty himself was the untranslatable unknown to Chingachgook. Yet across this unsuperable gulf in being there passed some strange communion between the two instances, invisible, intangible, unknowable—a quality of pure unknowable embrace. And out of this embrace arises the strange wing-covered seraph of new race-being. From this communion is procreated a new race-soul, which henceforth gestates within the living humanity of the West. (*SM* 103)

Readers since Lawrence's day, who know of the rise of fascist "organic" states and who justifiably eschew the doctrine of a "race-soul," must recoil from many of his political concepts. Lawrence modified or rejected some of them himself through ensuing years. But his ideas issue always from deeper sources than any political attitudes with which they may coincide, from time to time, as he finds meaningful symbols in the life of his day. In these essays he incorporates most of history—and its course for the future—within his vision of the natural sensual order of life. Much of his historiography must be understood as an attempt to correct the past—his own and mankind's—by understanding how men came to abhor their impulse to love other men.

The literary characters who enact the Puritanical repression of sensual life all reveal, to Lawrence, their unconscious drift toward death. The character of Leatherstocking shows the mad, great purposiveness of the soul that conquers itself and receives the shock of death. Leatherstocking is "the last instance of the integral, progressive, soul of the white man in America," Lawrence says. (*SM* 116) Cooper was entranced by the hidden meaning of the crusty old frontiersman who first appears in *The Pioneers*. He allowed the character to grow younger in successive novels, filling in an earlier life that shows Leatherstocking's initial spiritual triumph over the world of flesh and unconscious nature—which has become alien and spoiled in his last old-age adventures. Young Deerslayer's only remaining sensual passion is "for the experiences of danger and death":

> Ecstasy after ecstasy of keen peril and terrible death-dealing passes through his frame, gradually, mystically reducing him, dissolving out his animate tissue, the tissue of his oldness, into death as a pearl dissolves in wine. This is his slow, perfect, sensual consummation, his ultimate mystic consummation into death. For as an individual and as a race unit he must pass utterly into death —dissolve out.
>
> But even this is a process of futurity. It is the flower which burns down to mould, to liberate the new seed. And the lovely American landscape is the pure landscape of futurity: not of our present factory-smoked futurity, but of the true future of the as yet unborn, or scarcely born, race of Americans. (*SM* 111)

After Leatherstocking, American literature records "the long process of post-mortem activity in disintegration," as the white psyche, like a decomposing body, is reduced to the nullity "which *must* intervene between life-cycle and life-cycle." Poe's tales analytically examine the reductive process: "Poe is a man writhing in the mystery of his own undoing.

He is a great dead soul. . . . He leads us back, through pang after pang of disintegrative sensation, back towards the end of all things, where the beginning is." (*SM* 117) Significantly in regard to Lawrence's experience, he finds that Poe's preoccupation with family curses and the disfiguring of loved ones clarifies the actual destructiveness in "the stress of inordinate love . . . the consuming into a oneness." Love or hate, equally, can become a lust "to possess, or to be possessed by" the soul of another individual; and "this helpless craving for utter merging or identification" lies at the back of the incest-desire, Lawrence says. But incest itself is not a primal motive; it is only one of the manifestations of the desire to "transgress the bounds of being." For Lawrence the primal sin is the violation of the intact self; and he says that Poe's tales give lurid and melodramatic evidence of what really happens when independent identities are broken down by possessive love. "The triumph of love," he explains in a peroration, "lies in the communion of beings, who, in the very perfection of communion, recognise and allow the mutual otherness."

Lawrence cites the destructiveness of inordinate love in his examination of the works of Hawthorne also. "Hester Prynne is the successor of Ligeia," he says. (*SM* 141) Ligeia died with a shriek of madness and claimed her ultimate victim only from the vantage of her return from death. Hester is not so completely badgered. Living within a world of total sensual repression, a Puritan community, and subjected to the spiritual effulgence of Arthur Dimmesdale, part of her nevertheless "turns in rich, lurid revenge." Hester rouses and possesses Dimmesdale's sensual soul and destroys his spiritual manliness. Yet she remains outwardly submissive, private and exotic—like Gudrun, really—while through the years of their secret guilt she undermines an era by her unconscious, malevolent

sensual mastery over "the triumphant spiritual being in man."
The Puritans are halfway right to regard her as a witch, and
with symbolic appropriateness Hester remains the wife and
unwilling accomplice of ancient Chillingworth, the diabolic
wizard of black arts and sensual mysteries.

Hawthorne worshipped Hester, Lawrence claims, even as
the Puritan community worship her on their scaffold, for
being a dark, sensual creature tainted with sin and an " 'oriental' " voluptuousness. Consciously, he adopts an attitude of
ethical judgment against her because he speaks for the repression of spontaneous nature and he fears the symbolic
meaning of the Black Man who lives in the encircling forest.
But the unconscious Hawthorne who is the artist and not the
moralist longs "for revenge, even upon himself. He is divided
against himself. Openly he stands for the upper, spiritual, reasoned being. Secretly he lusts in the sensual imagination, in
bruising the heel of this spiritual self and laming it for ever.
All his reasoned exposition is a pious fraud, kept up to satisfy
his own upper or outward self." (*SM* 141) Partly because of
the disparity between what the author felt and what he understood, *The Scarlet Letter* is "a profound and wonderful
book, one of the eternal revelations":

> It is the lasting representative book of American litera-
> ture. If it displeases us in any particular, it is in the way
> the ethical Hawthorne embroiders over the artist Haw-
> thorne. The deepest joy is the pride of sin: and all the
> preaching is so lugubrious and moral. This touch of cant
> or falseness, duplicity, is however absolutely essential to
> the fallen Puritan psyche, and therefore artistically true.
> The lust of sin goes simultaneous with the solemn con-
> demnation of sin. Which is peculiarly American. And
> this book is the myth of the fallen Puritan psyche, in the
> New World. (*SM* 168–69)

The essays on Poe and Hawthorne bring Lawrence to an extended judgment against the Magna Mater in American life whose chaotic love destroys the male, who has lost his sexual leadership. "Through two thousand years man, the leader, has been slaying the dragon of the primary self, the sensual psyche, and the woman has been with him. But the hour of triumph is the hour of the end. In the hour of triumph the slain rises up in revenge and the destroyer is destroyed." Having no further mystic vision to sustain him individually, man falls emptied at the feet of woman, and Lawrence says that her repressed sensuality invariably breaks out to seize him:

> The deep, subconscious, primary self in woman recoils in antagonism. But it is a recoil of long, secret destructiveness, nihilism, subtle, serpent-like, outwardly submissive. . . .
>
> With all her passion she cherishes and nourishes her man, and yet her cherishing and nourishing only destroy him more. With all her soul she tries to save life. And the greatness of her effort only further saps the root of life, weakens the soul of man, destroys him, and drives him into an insanity of self-destruction. Such is the Age of Woman. Such it always has been, and always will be. It is the age of cowardly, false, destructive men. It is the age of fatal, suffocating love, love which kills like a Laocoon snake.
>
> Woman cannot take the creative lead; she can only give the creative radiation. From her as from Eve must come the first suggestion or impulse of new being. When, however, she recoils from man's leadership and takes matters in her own hands, she recoils in mystic destruction. She cannot make a beginning, go on ahead. She can only prompt man, not knowing herself to what she prompts him. . . .
>
> It is the fate of woman, that what she is she is darkly and helplessly. What woman *knows*, she knows because

man has taught it to her. What she *is*, this is another matter. She can never give expression to the profound movements of her own being. These movements can only find an expression through a man. Man is the utterer, woman is the first cause. Whatever God there is made it so. (*SM* 143–45)

With this Miltonic pronouncement that fixes woman in a subordinate, governed role, Lawrence moves from considering the sexes' relationship to considering man's relation with cosmic elements. After Hawthorne, he says, the male adventurer in the unknown avoids the corrupted sensual principle in woman and turns, like Dana and Melville, to discover the sea. But the sea is his elemental mother, and he flees headlong to his further disintegration. Dana in *Two Years Before The Mast* triumphs over the hostile forces of nature by making every sensual experience perfectly conscious and known. Only two moments of deep, spontaneous passion elude his complete understanding and controlled response: his impotent rage against the tyrannical captain, and his impulse of love for the native boy, Hope. "Hope is for a moment to Dana what Chingachgook is to Cooper—the hearts-brother, the answerer. But only for an ephemeral moment." The rest of his experience is the inexorable advance of idealism and consciousness into the mysteries of the sea.

But no one, Lawrence says, surpasses Melville for carrying conscious awareness beyond the shores and away from the usual centers of human life: "The greatest seer and poet of the sea, perhaps in all the world, is Herman Melville." (*SM* 219) As he appears to Lawrence in *Typee* and *Omoo* Melville resembles a beachcombing Gerald Crich, unconsciously always seeking to quench his spirit in water and coldness. Even in the midst of his South Seas sensual paradise he is

compelled by his relentless will, that is "always clinched, forcing life in some direction or other." At the end of his potential
as a tormented idealist, Melville tries to reduce himself; he is
like the decomposing corpse of Poe's soul, or Gerald's, drain-
ing down to its material composition:

> Melville makes the great return. He would really melt
> himself, an elemental, back into his vast beloved ele-
> ment, material though it is. All his fire he would carry
> down, quench in the sea. It is time for the sea to receive
> back her own, into the pale, bluish underworld of the
> watery after-life. He is like a Viking going home to the
> sea, encumbered with age and memories, and a sort of
> accomplished despair, almost madness. The great North-
> ern cycle of which he is the returning unit has com-
> pleted its round, accomplished itself, flowered from the
> waters like forget-me-nots and sea-poppies, and now re-
> turns into the sea, giving back its consciousness and its
> being to the vast material element, burying its flames in
> the deeps, self-conscious and deliberate. (*SM* 220)

Ahab is the completed symbol in American literature of
monomaniac, ideal purposiveness pitted fatally against the
vestiges of sensual spontaneity in the self, which are symbolized in the white whale, "the last warm-blooded tenant of the
waters." (*SM* 235) *Moby-Dick* is "a book of exoteric symbolism of profound significance," Lawrence says, "and of considerable tiresomeness." It is always on the verge of falsity, because "Melville tries to square himself with the intellectual
world by dragging in deliberate transcendentalism, deliberate
symbols and 'deeper meanings.' All this is insufferably clumsy
and in clownish bad taste." But what he renders perfectly,
Lawrence says, are the effects that are nearest his sympathy
for "the sheer naked slidings of the elements, and the curious
cause-and-effect of material events." These he registers "in

sheer physical, vibrational sensitiveness, like a marvellous wireless-station. . . . And he records also, almost beyond pain or pleasure, the extreme transitions of the isolated, far-driven soul, the soul which is now alone, without human connection." Only one human being enters Melville's soul, and that is Queequeg, whom Ishmael actually loves, but Melville disguises his love with intellectualizing. (*SM* 237–38)

The symbolic whale that Melville tracks down, Whitman at last captures, Lawrence states in his concluding chapter. "The pure sensual body of man, at its deepest remoteness and intensity, this is the White Whale. And this is what Whitman captures." (*SM* 259–60) He alone transcended his individual being and he identifies himself completely with the abstract identity of democratic Man, *"en masse."* He conquered his passional nature and subdued it in spiritual, deliberate love, effacing the bounds of being and achieving his infinitude. There is no going beyond him—except to begin the next stage of living, the resurrection of the sensual being. And this impulse, too, appears delicately tinged with newness in *Leaves of Grass*. Whitman's wistful celebration of "the mystery of manly love, the love of comrades" heralds the resurgence of sensual communion among men that will build an organic society:

> Continually he tells us the same truth: the new world will be built upon the love of comrades, the new great dynamic of life will be manly love. Out of this inspiration the creation of the future.
>
> The strange Calamus has its pink-tinged root by the pond, and it sends up its leaves of comradeship, comrades at one root, without the intervention of woman, the female. This comradeship is to be the final cohering principle of the new world, the new Democracy. It is the cohering principle of perfect soldiery, as he tells in

"Drum Taps." It is the cohering principle of final *unison* in creative activity. And it is extreme and alone, touching the confines of death. It is something terrible to bear, terrible to be responsible for. . . .

And what is the responsibility? It is for the new great era of mankind. And upon what is this new era established? On the perfect circuits of vital flow between human beings. First, the great sexless normal relation between individuals, simple sexless friendships, unison of family, and clan, and nation, and group. Next, the powerful sex relation between man and woman, culminating in the eternal orbit of marriage. And, finally, the sheer friendship, the love between comrades, the manly love which alone can create a new era of life. (*SM* 261–63)

The entire series of essays is carefully structured to lead to this conclusion. The essays retell a story of progressive emotional degeneration in the modern world that is also the story of *Women in Love,* but with this difference of a happy conclusion that Lawrence manages to foresee in American life. The bond of manly love that Birkin could not effectively establish with Gerald is positively initiated in Whitman. The destructiveness of sexual love in which the woman is sensually dominant and possessive, as in Gerald's and Gudrun's affair, is roundly denounced and taken care of by simple condemnation. The impulse for creative renewal in all of life, that in the novel came fraily and ambiguously only from Ursula, is ascribed in these essays to the "pure daimon" of the continent, the inexhaustible sensual vitality of the landscape that infused the "subtlest plasm" of the new world settlers. From his reading of American literature Lawrence interpreted a meaning which seems to solve the problems of life that he uncovered in his greatest but most pessimistic novel. His "philosophy" imposed a happier gloss over his insight to his fictional characters, and perhaps that is another reason why Lawrence felt that it was so terribly urgent to write these essays immediately after he finished the novel. His aim was not critical evaluation or historical thoroughness; he wished mainly to gather sufficient evidence for the reconfirmation of his hope. He speaks of Whitman in tones of gratitude and sustained praise because Whitman passionately claimed that the hope of future civilization lies in perfecting manly love, which is what Lawrence also was trying to believe. For both visionaries, that liberating change in man's sensual experience was destined to occur in America.

Just how narrowly he selected his material in these essays to fit his argument is evident by what he neglected to consider. He dealt with writers who seemed unequivocally to bear out his thesis, and he neglected those whose art or chronology did not support his purpose in writing. Two major writers are not even discussed: there is no mention of Emerson or Thoreau, even though the title originally planned for the series was "The Transcendental Element in American Literature." Lawrence knew their works well and he had once been ecstatic about *Walden.*[2] Though the essays are propagandistic in this respect, they nevertheless contain extraordinary literary criticism—and it is more cogently expressed than in the version of the essays that was later published as a book. Lawrence acutely perceives the structural complexity and the tonal nuances of the works that he considers, and his sensitivity to the authors' underlying emotions helps to make the writers' sensibilities immediate and coherent to the reader. More successfully than any critic of his time, he treated formal literary qualities in relation to the individual life and the social ethos of the artist. It is an especial loss to the criticism of American literature that he wrote no essay on

Thoreau, for whom he surely had deep sympathy, nor on Emerson, whose idiom and concepts often strikingly resemble his own.

The relevance of the essays to Lawrence's subsequent work is that they create a symbolic global geography, establishing America as the point of inevitable crisis in the next development of consciousness. He invested the locality with much of his deepest intuition about the self, particularly about himself. In doing so, he made his imagination dependent, to a large degree, upon the continuing inspiration of the American continent. He strove thereafter to realize consciously the meaning of the place that he had encoded with personal significance. The attitude toward America which he carried forward from these studies for several years and through many works is, understandably enough, proprietary, hierophantic, and illusional. In a very intimate sense, it is *his* country.

Lawrence's references to present-day Indians show how he immediately began to use details of actual life in the United States as a way of representing the psychic drama in the self. Because they are customarily identified with the natural state of the continent, Indians became for Lawrence images of the sensuality which white men have repressed in their natures. He saw them also quite literally as primitives whose level of life has long been surpassed and who now survive feebly with a hopelessly corrupted culture, but their plight within the constriction of America's industrial civilization was living evidence of white men's disintegrating sensuality. Therefore, a possible way to renew mankind in America, as Lawrence reasoned within the logic of his symbols, is to revalue the Indian's quality of being and incorporate it within present life.

In an article entitled "America, Listen to Your Own,"

Lawrence exhorted the United States through the pages of *The New Republic* to acknowledge that the American forefathers were repressing their own sensuality when they nearly annihilated aboriginal life; modern Americans should "pick up the life-thread where the mysterious Red race let it fall." By taking inspiration from a way of experience that has been denied its fruition and by fulfilling its potentials, Americans could liberate a fuller range of their human capacities. It was absurd, he commented with reference to tourists in Italy, for Americans to feel abject and wonder-struck over the monuments and traditions of Europe; European culture is a finished product, but the future for America lies in the redemption and continuance of the unfinished, unperfected past that fell with the red man. If Americans would accept the aboriginal spirit of the continent they would reverse the drift of their repressive European consciousness and find themselves turning to a new morality and experiencing a new range of feelings:

> America must turn again to catch the spirit of her own dark, aboriginal continent.
> That which was abhorrent to the Pilgrim Fathers and to the Spaniards, that which was called the Devil, the black Demon of savage America, this great aboriginal spirit the Americans must recognize again, recognize and embrace. The devil and anathema of our forefathers hides the Godhead which we seek.[3]

In an article written for the *New York Times* Lawrence tried again to arouse interest in Indian culture as a creative influence which could shape the future. The Indians, he argued, can offer modern man no model for living but they can awaken into consciousness parts of the self that have been denied in modern European and American culture; and "one moment of reconciliation between the white spirit and the dark" could turn the course of civilization toward a fuller realization of the individual:

> The Indians keep burning an eternal fire, the sacred fire of the old dark religion. To the vast white America, either in our generation or in time of our children or grandchildren, will come some fearful convulsion. Some terrible convulsion will take place among the millions of this country, sooner or later. When the pueblos are gone. But oh, let us have the grace and dignity to shelter these ancient centres of life, so that, if die they must, they die a natural death. And at the same time, let us try to adjust ourselves again to the Indian outlook, to take up an old dark thread from their vision, and see again as they see, without forgetting we are ourselves.
>
> For it is a new era we have now got to cross into. And our electric light won't show us over the gulf. We have to feel our way by the dark thread of the old vision. Before it lapses, let us take it up.[4]

Lawrence preached to Americans and, probably, he anticipated a large popular following for his ideas among them. Seeing America as a symbol for the self, he felt drawn—even obligated—to participate in the current life of the country and to influence personally the national destiny. Within six months after the Armistice, which was as soon as he and Frieda were likely to obtain new passports, Lawrence made plans to emigrate to the United States. He expected to earn money and renown by giving lectures, and he counted heavily on the support of Amy Lowell to help him through the period of resettlement. Perhaps she would allow him to reside with her "for a week or two, if I can't provide for myself just at the very first," he wrote. Amy Lowell sent a barrage of letters to Lawrence and separately to Frieda, urging them not to come. She believed his plans were unrealistic; he did not have an accurate idea of the prejudice against his books in America, where libraries kept even *Sons and Lovers* in a locked case, she pointed out. She did not think that he would get many lecture engagements. It was all lamentable, she told him, but "I think you are a big enough fellow to know that I write you a letter like this because I want you to know the facts of the case as they really are." [5]

Dissuaded by her and opposed by Frieda, who intended to visit Germany and who was not keen on leaving Europe, Lawrence sailed from England in November 1919—not for America but en route to Italy. For three more years, he vacillated in his decision "to transfer all my life to America," while he accumulated new reasons to take the final step and dismissed old reasons for hesitation. The extremes of anticipation and of aversion which mark his long-deliberated approach to the United States indicate how much of his inner life with its intense dialectics of negation and hope he had invested in the image of America. The difficulty in acting upon his resolution to go there was partly the difficulty of facing the most personal and troubling issues that lay behind its symbolic attraction for him.

5

"A world of perilous, pure freedom"

For the rest of his life Lawrence was a traveler, sojourning among places that failed to hold him, but examining with great interest the lives of parochial or primitive peoples wherever he traveled. Moving restlessly from one part of the earth to another, he looked for social forms of male camaraderie. He expected to find signs of unconscious bonds of fellowship among cultures which appeared to offer a broader range of emotional expression than the English. Through the wander years he returned to England reluctantly for brief, unhappy visits. His main circuit lay in a southeastward trek around the world, from the Mediterranean through the Pacific to the American Southwest and back to the Mediterranean, where he died in southern France in 1930. Leaving England in November 1919, he traveled first in Italy until Frieda rejoined him after her depressing visit to postwar Germany. They lived on Capri for two months, amidst the caviling, arty Anglo community that Lawrence could not bear any longer than that. They moved to Sicily and rented the upper floor of a farmhouse, the Fontana Vecchia, which was their home for the next two years. Though they made excursions to Sardinia and Malta and took extended summer trips back to the Continent, Taormina was one of the places where Lawrence settled for a significant time. But he moved on in 1922 to Ceylon, to Australia, and to the United States and Mexico.

Most of his writing during this period is neglected or denigrated by readers whose interest in Lawrence is limited to his major novels, since *Aaron's Rod* and *Kangaroo* are accurately regarded as inferior to his earlier fiction. He also completed *The Lost Girl,* which even he considered a potboiler—though, ironically, it won him the only prize and official recognition that came in his lifetime.[1] But his other work of this time is more notable. He made his final revisions of "The Fox" and he wrote several other short stories, including "The Captain's Doll" and "The Horse Dealer's Daughter." He elaborated the concepts of psychology that were advanced in his first essays on American writers, and produced two books of biopsychic theory,[2] *Psychoanalysis and the Unconscious* and *Fantasia of the Unconscious.* He wrote a long, artful Introduction to aid the sale of *Memoirs of the Foreign Legion,* by Maurice Magnus, and it deserves to be treated as a companion piece to his best travel book, *Sea and Sardinia,* also of this period. He wrote his best single volume of poetry, *Birds, Beasts and Flowers;* and arriving in America, he immediately sketched Indian life in memorable essays and he entirely rewrote his *Studies in Classic American Literature,* which has since proved to be the most influential piece of criticism written on the subject. The creative production of the four years between his departure and his first return visit to England is a large portion of Lawrence's work—and its characteristics point toward the imminent crisis of his life's effort in art.

During this period Lawrence was encountering wholly

new and often exotic scenes and giving detailed accounts of
his travels. In his fiction and non-fiction alike, he describes
with considerable documentary and journalistic interest a
contemporary objective world that is unfamiliar and curious
to him. Peoples' costumes and their habitual or "racial" gestures, a city's statues, its suburbs, its newspaper features, the
price of food, the way that roads are, the view at a famous
spot, the characteristics of the natives, the peasants, or the vil-
lagers: details of this order convey a travelogue of foreign
lands. And standing in the midst of the scenes, observed and
commented upon as if he is part of the view that is being described, or sometimes turning to address the reader directly as
if in private conversation about the scene at hand, there is
usually the identified figure of Lawrence himself as a character appearing in the imaginative world of his own writings.

Sometimes, his presence as a seemingly artless, candid
writer adds to the reportorial immediacy of his observations;
he shows himself amidst his subject, like an eyewitness on the
spot. But sometimes his authorial presence is merely self-
advertising in a juvenile or compulsive manner, and his rhetorical foolery interferes with our attention to the narrative, the
characters, the description or the argument. In both cases,
however, Lawrence's self-dramatizations reveal his sense of
detachment from his inner life; throughout this period he
writes from a distant, ironic perspective that pictures rather
than directly expresses himself. The rhetorical mode suggests
his aversion or separation from the undercurrents of his consciousness, and the occasional passages of resumed expressionism are momentary and intensely painful to him.

Implicit self-dramatization is, of course, part of his profoundest creative impulse, and it is evident in his early auto-

biographical work and in *Women in Love* as well. But the explicit characterization of himself as part of the objective world that is observed in his writings becomes prominent only after Lawrence left England and undertook his "savage pilgrimage," as he once called his years of wandering. As if drawn by a "magnetic current" such as he postulated in *Symbolic Meaning*, he submitted to the feeling that his travels were destined. He believed that traveling aided his self-discovery and fulfillment; in *Aaron's Rod* Lawrence asserts through his persona, Rawdon Lilly, that "a new place brings out a new thing in a man." But Lawrence also felt deep regret over the loss of a stationary center of attachment such as England had been, and after many removals to new places he complained about his alienation from himself. In a letter to Catherine Carswell, Lawrence wrote after three years of traveling: "Perhaps it is necessary for me to try these places, perhaps it is my destiny to know the world. It only excites the outside of me. The inside it leaves more isolated and stoic than ever. That's how it is. It is all a form of running away from oneself and the great problems." At that moment he had arrived in the United States, and he was reviling it as a nation of egoistic willfulness and self-conscious posturing. The world of people disappointed and exacerbated him everywhere he went; his confrontation with humanity became less and less significant. In the same letter to Mrs. Carswell, he adds: "Only the desert has a fascination—to ride alone—in the sun in the for ever unpossessed country—away from man. That is a great temptation, because one rather hates mankind nowadays." (*CL* 723–24) But before Lawrence did, in effect, ride into that desert and realize the temptation which it signified, he wrote himself into a state of utter withdrawal from a commonly experienced world. The self-dramatizing mode in his works records his progressive devaluing of outer reality and his venturing away into psychological isolation.

In *Aaron's Rod* and *Kangaroo* Lawrence is represented both as an authorial voice, confiding and expostulating with his "dear reader," and as a character who is a small, chirpy, irascible, half-comical man. As Rawdon Lilly or as Lovatt Somers, the Lawrence persona pursues through travel and writing the same investigations of life that engaged Lawrence in England, Italy, and Australia while he wrote the novels. He is a restless figure who is impelled by whim or the slightest occasion to abandon one living-place after another. Yet he believes in the imminent possibility of a stable personal and societal life, and he would like to assume a leading role in a movement or party to initiate the new order. With his cronies he tirelessly discusses love, marriage, and social reconstruction based on manly love and leadership. At *Kaffeklatschen* in Florence or political meetings in Sydney, the fascinating but stagey dialogues give the reader an impression of overhearing the author's recent conversations with his acquaintances. Like Lawrence, the persona recognizes that his social impulse is frustrated by his skepticism and his terrible insight to other people's motives for action. Regarding his own motives, each persona is continually subject to criticism and ridicule from his indomitable wife, as Lawrence was often challenged by Frieda in their notorious conflicts. The reader is urged to recognize the similarities between the fictional and the real couple by the unmistakable, deliberate caricature in the descriptions of man and wife. In all, the thinly veiled disguise thrown revealingly about himself keeps us mindful that the fiction we are reading is chiefly the fictionalized immediate experience of the author, as Lawrence wishes it to be known.

In *Aaron's Rod* the Lawrence persona is a secondary though not a minor character. He is a socially obscure but charismatic figure to whom Aaron Sisson is drawn after he leaves his wife and children in the Midlands because domestic life came to an end for him—as naturally and inexplicably as birth or death, he says. The first two chapters which show Aaron brooding in Beldover before taking flight are among the best passages Lawrence wrote in the realistic manner of *Sons and Lovers*. But soon the author intrudes to break the spell of pure fiction and to insist upon the actuality of his personal hand in the contrivance of novel writing. He joshes the reader and frets about the difficulty of getting his diverse characters assembled and his story under way. After the opening chapters, Aaron's experience through the novel—some of which would seem unlikely, at best—is made fictitious by the author's continual confidences to the reader. When Aaron in Italy finally considers the deep causes of his estrangement from his wife, the psychological immediacy of this important passage is repeatedly undercut by the authorial voice:

> Thoughts something in this manner ran through Aaron's subconscious mind as he sat still in the strange house. He could not have fired it all off at any listener, as these pages are fired off at any chance reader. Nevertheless there it was, risen to half consciousness in him.
>
> . . . .
>
> Don't grumble at me then, gentle reader, and swear at me that this damned fellow wasn't half clever enough to think all these smart things, and realise all these fine-drawn-out-subtleties. You are quite right, he wasn't, yet it all resolved itself in him as I say, and it is for you to prove that it didn't. (XIII)

Yet, the author's asides and cajolery are often amusing, like clever conversation. When Aaron is led to his guest-room up the grand staircase of a palatial villa into a further, modest stairway beyond a little door, Lawrence observes the irony: "Man can so rarely keep it up all the way, the grandeur." His voice maintains the generally light tone of the novel. It is a book that one must read with detachment and a willingness to be diverted from the fiction to the anterior, "real" world in which the author works and offers his own personality for attention. We are not allowed to accept Aaron's story with willing suspension of our disbelief; and for this reason it is all the easier to recognize in Rawdon Lilly the figure of Lawrence himself.

Lilly speaks authoritatively about how people should live. He argues with a knighted British philanthropist that man should rid himself of individual economic purpose and live with trust in Providence. Among a group of jaded and effeminate men, he agrees with their analysis of marriage and their condemnation of modern woman for being sexually possessive. In a political discussion that includes a Jewish socialist and a crusty Scottish reactionary, Lilly argues like a fascist, and then adopts a palatable vagueness about the integrity of individuals:

> "I agree in the rough with Argyle. You've got to have a sort of slavery again. People are not *men:* they are insects and instruments, and their destiny is slavery. They are too many for me, and so what I think is ineffectual. But ultimately they will be brought to agree— after sufficient extermination—and then they will elect for themselves a proper and healthy and energetic slavery."
>
> "I should like to know what you mean by slavery [Levison asks]. Because to me it is impossible that slavery should be healthy and energetic. You seem to have

some other idea in your mind, and you merely use the word slavery out of exasperation—"

"I mean it none the less. I mean a real committal of the life-issue of inferior beings to the responsibility of a superior being."

"It'll take a bit of knowing, who are the inferior and which is the superior," said Levison sarcastically.

"Not a bit. It is written between a man's brows, which he is."

"I'm afraid we shall all read differently."

"So long as we're liars."

"And putting that question aside: I presume that you mean that this committal of the life-issue of inferior beings to someone higher shall be made voluntarily—a sort of voluntary self-gift of the inferiors—"

"Yes—more or less—and a voluntary acceptance. For it's no pretty gift, after all.—But once made it must be held fast by genuine power. Oh yes—no playing and fooling about with it. Permanent and very efficacious power."

"You mean military power?"

"I do, of course."

Here Levison smiled a long, slow, subtle smile of ridicule. It all seemed to him the preposterous pretentiousness of a megalomaniac—one whom, after a while, humanity would probably have the satisfaction of putting into prison, or into a lunatic asylum. And Levison felt strong, overwhelmingly strong, in the huge social power with which he, insignificant as he was, was armed against such criminal-imbecile pretensions as those above set forth. Prison or the lunatic asylum. The face of the fellow gloated in these two inevitable engines of his disapproval.

"It will take you some time before you'll get your doctrines accepted," he said.

"Accepted! I'd be sorry. I don't want a lot of swine snouting and sniffling at me with their acceptance.—

Bah, Levison—one can easily make a fool of you. Do you take this as my gospel?"

"I take it you are speaking seriously."

Here Lilly broke into that peculiar, gay, whimsical smile.

"But I should say the blank opposite with just as much fervour," he declared.

"Do you mean to say you don't *mean* what you've been saying?" said Levison, now really looking angry.

"Why, I'll tell you the real truth," said Lilly. "I think every man is a sacred and holy individual, *never* to be violated. I think there is only one thing I hate to the verge of madness, and that is *bullying*. To see any living creature *bullied*, in *any* way, almost makes a murderer of me. That is true. Do you believe it—?"

"Yes," said Levison unwillingly. "That may be true as well. You have no doubt, like most of us, got a complex nature which—" (XX)

At that moment of possible resolution to the debate, an anarchist's bomb explodes in the café where they are sitting and the scene of bloodshed and indiscriminate destruction is the emblematic conclusion to the conflict of ideologies. Lawrence dreaded the resurgence of war; yet, as a man preternaturally sensitive to the violence in the life of his era, he acknowledged in himself the attitudes that were soon articulated by the fascists, and for a time he accepted the recourse to totalitarianism that swept over Europe.[3] Even his ironic treatment of Levison prophetically belittles the confidence in rationality that blinded his era's liberals.

For Lawrence the political reorganization of life would be valuable only as a procedure for liberating the sensual man from the bonds of an overly rationalistic culture. Aaron Sisson's malaise is not the result of social or economic conditions; his emotional illness indicates a sensual failure within his private world of narrowly domestic experience. He feels that his soul has been broken into and violated by the possessiveness and dependency of his wife, whose idea of marriage is "that the highest her man could ever know or ever reach, was to be perfectly enveloped in her all-beneficent love." (XIII) After Aaron leaves her, he comes to understand that he is rejecting the principle of the marriage relationship in which he was expected to repudiate his "intrinsic and central aloneness." This kind of threat against his integrity disrupts his marriage and more of such love saps his power to live, for when Aaron is later seduced by a young woman, he falls ill and becomes mordantly dejected. Only Lilly—who believes in his own superior grace to govern life in lesser beings—can revive Aaron's will to recover health. Lilly apparently transfers his vitality into Aaron's body by entrancedly rubbing him with oil until he shows signs of "regaining himself." With his life-rousing, "mindless" rubbing of Aaron's "lower body," Lilly claims Aaron's allegiance to his power. By submitting to the authority of a greater male soul, Aaron could extricate himself from woman's fixed conception of love, and he would come into full possession of his own nature. Aaron, however, finds it difficult to comprehend and trust an allegiance with masculine power.

In Lilly's parting words to Aaron, Lawrence delivers his analysis of unrest among individuals in postwar Europe and he prescribes a political solution that most of Europe adopted —but which Lawrence soon rejected after testing his social philosophy in the imaginative world of his writings and finding its ideas ultimately repellent. The kind of social organization that he prescribed for the liberation of man's varied sensuality could not be achieved by mere political means, however extreme, and Lawrence gradually dismissed his belief in totalitarian order. In the final passage of *Aaron's Rod*, however, the despair and devaluation of life that underlie the novel's ironic levity emerge clearly in the form of doctrines that were to dominate a sick world:

> "I told you there were two urges—two great life-urges, didn't I? There may be more. But it comes on me so strongly, now, that there are two: love, and power. And we've been trying to work ourselves, at least as individuals, from the love-urge exclusively, hating the power-urge, and repressing it. And now I find we've got to accept the very thing we've hated.
>
> "We've exhausted our love-urge, for the moment. And yet we try to force it to continue working. So we get inevitably anarchy and murder. It's no good. We've got to accept the power motive, accept it in deep responsibility, do you understand me? It is a great life motive. It was that great dark power-urge which kept Egypt so intensely living for so many centuries. It is a vast dark source of life and strength in us now, waiting either to issue into true action, or to burst into cataclysm. Power—the power-urge. The will-to-power —but not in Nietzsche's sense. Not intellectual power. Not mental power. Not conscious will-power. Not even wisdom. But dark, living fructifying power. . . .
>
> ". . . . That's where Nietzsche was wrong. His was the conscious and benevolent will, in fact, the love-will. But the deep power-urge is not conscious of its aims: and it is certainly not consciously benevolent or love-directed. . . .
>
> ". . . . The mode of our being is such that we can only live and have our being whilst we are implicit in one of the great dynamic modes. We *must* either love, or rule. And once the love-mode changes, as change it must, for we are worn out and becoming evil in its persistence, then the other mode will take place in us. And there will be profound, profound obedience in

place of this love-crying, obedience to the incalculable
power-urge. And men must submit to the greater soul in
a man, for their guidance: and women must submit to
the positive power-soul in man, for their being."

"You'll never get it," said Aaron.

"You will, when all men want it. All men say, they
want a leader. Then let them in their souls *submit* to
some greater soul than theirs. At present, when they say
they want a leader, they mean they want an instrument,
like Lloyd George. A mere instrument for their use. But
it's more than that. It's the reverse. It's the deep, fathom-
less submission to the heroic soul in a greater man. You,
Aaron, you too have the need to submit. You, too, have
the need livingly to yield to a more heroic soul, to give
yourself. You know you have. And you know it isn't
love. It is life-submission. And you know it. But you
kick against the pricks. And perhaps you'd rather die
than yield. And so, die you must. It is your affair."

There was a long pause. Then Aaron looked up into
Lilly's face. It was dark and remote-seeming. It was like
a Byzantine eikon at the moment.

"And whom shall I submit to?" he said.

"Your soul will tell you," replied the other. (XXI)

By comparing Lilly to a Byzantine eikon Lawrence means
to suggest a holy power evident in his intent face, and the
novel concludes with this image of Lawrence proposing that
men must die or submit their souls to persons like himself.
The egomania of the final pages overcomes the author's irony
that is the viewpoint through most of the book. The apotheosis of Lilly is an embarrassment to the reader, and perhaps it
was also to Lawrence at some level of consciousness; for while
finishing *Aaron's Rod* he was taking another glance at himself
in *Sea and Sardinia*,[4] and in that book he sees a limited, half-
comical, wholly mortal man—whose attractiveness is only in
his subtle awareness of life, including his self-awareness.

Sea and Sardinia is the record of a ten-day excursion that he took with Frieda in January 1921 from their residence in Taormina. Lawrence's restiveness is the keynote of the book, announced in the elliptical first sentences: "Comes over one an absolute necessity to move. And what is more, to move in some particular direction." As they travel by train, ship, and bus, like postwar tourists going from Sicily through Sardinia and back, Lawrence repeatedly longs to take flight, to sail forever, to go along the open road and never stop. The clear mornings over the sea rouse his spirit for endless sauntering; to one burdened with his mortal sameness, dawn on the Tyrrhenian brings "the glad lonely wringing of the heart":

> Not to be clogged to the land any more. Not to be any more like a donkey with a log on its leg, fastened to weary earth that has no answer now. But to be off.
>
> To find three masculine, world-lost souls, and, world-lost, saunter and saunter on along with them, across the dithering space, as long as life lasts! Why come to anchor? There is nothing to anchor for. Land has no answer to the soul any more. It has gone inert. Give me a ship, kind gods, and three world-lost comrades. Hear me! And let me wander aimless across this vivid oyster world, the world empty of man, where space flies happily. (45–46)

It is implacable Mt. Etna towering on the horizon that drives him away from Fontana Vecchia, Lawrence explains. Elaborately, he personifies the volcano as a timeless witch, a perennial Circe, whose commanding attractiveness threatens to possess men's souls and leave whole races abject in her power. The feminine meaning of Mt. Etna has broken the masculinity, he says, of all the Mediterannean nations:

> Ah, what a mistress, this Etna! with her strange winds prowling round her like Circe's panthers, some black,

some white. With her strange, remote communications and her terrible dynamic exhalations. She makes men mad. Such terrible vibrations of wicked and beautiful electricity she throws about her, like a deadly net! Nay, sometimes, verily, one can feel a new current of her demon magnetism seize one's living tissue and change the peaceful life of one's active cells. She makes a storm in the living plasm and a new adjustment. And sometimes it is like a madness.

This timeless Grecian Etna, in her lower-heaven loveliness, so lovely, so lovely, what a torture! Not many men can really stand her without losing their souls. She is like Circe. Unless a man is very strong, she takes his soul away from him and leaves him not a beast, but an elemental creature, intelligent and soulless. Intelligent, almost inspired, and soulless, like the Etna Sicilians. Intelligent daimons, and humanly, according to us, the most stupid people on earth. Ach, horror! How many men, how many races, has Etna put to flight? It was she who broke the quick of the Greek soul. And after the Greeks, she gave the Romans, the Normans, the Arabs, the Spaniards, the French, the Italians, even the English, she gave them all their inspired hour and broke their souls. (2)

The hyperbolic rhetoric that is almost totally non-descriptive initiates the serious, formal "plot" that governs his account of the journey. Lawrence hankers for spontaneous passional adventure as a respite from the self-awareness that is sometimes "like a madness." The heightened state of consciousness is attributed to the influence of an *eternal woman.* Like Miriam in *Sons and Lovers,* or Lydia Lawrence with her son, the feminine Mt. Etna inspires men to a peak of feeling but leaves them powerless, and Lawrence wants to escape from that trap. The irony of the Sardinian excursion is that in his quest for spontaneous experience, he grows only more mindful that the life of sensual communion is lost in the past.

At the end of the journey, he survives alone and grieving in a devalued world, much like Paul Morel after his mother's death, or like Birkin after Gerald's.

But it is the author's perceptions of outward things in kaleidoscopic vividness that take the foreground of this travel book, so unguardedly and gaily written. With a knapsack of personal articles and a "kitchenino" of utensils, Lawrence and Frieda, "the queen-bee," set off like vacationeers, keenly excited in the early morning that is dark and silent around them as they lock up their house and hurry down the hill to the depot. With wit and boyish fascination, Lawrence makes a romantic adventure out of the train's delay, or the meals on the tiny steamer, or the dinner at an inn shared with some conspiratorial, "soup-sucking" socialists. The bus across Sardinia is driven by moody Sardinians whom he sees as caricatures of young Hamlet and Jane Eyre's Mr. Rochester. A traveling huckster, a degenerate *giravago*, reminds him of a fallen knight-errant. Lawrence's perceptions add color and complexity to every incident. The reader can see the actual squalor and tedium of the journey, but only at the edges of the author's consciousness where stark objectivity remains untransformed by the artist's response. Yet it is there, the bleakness in the hills of Sardinia, the decay of human feeling in scenes of peasant solitariness, the pathos of this outworn and forgotten arena of life, and all the degrading bitterness of the recent war festering in people's souls, spilling out in unconscious insults to the volatile little Englishman with his odd beard, his knapsack, and his German wife. The romance and brilliance that the reader enjoys in following this excursion center in the figure of Lawrence alone, and the immediacy of his account is heightened precisely by the way that our sympathies must cling to his image amidst the forlornness or the chaos where he guides us. He brings life where he has come in search of it.

The creative spontaneity among men which Lawrence found nowhere in Sardinia he encounters in Palermo on his return journey, but only in a puppet show about Roland. The legend of medieval heroism dramatizes the values that he sought to recover in his restive sauntering:

> the massive, brilliant, outflinging recklessness in the male soul, summed up in the sudden word; *Andiamo!* Andiamo! Let us go on. Andiamo!—let us go hell knows where, but let us go on. The splendid recklessness and passion that knows no precept and no school-teacher, whose very molten spontaneity is its own guide. (202)

In the theater, where only men and boys are admitted, Lawrence enjoys the male comaraderie, and he watches with absolute delight as the Paladins overcome the magic of the evil witch:

> The old witch with her grey hair and staring eyes, succeeds in being ghastly. With just a touch, she would be a tall, benevolent old lady. But listen to her. Hear her horrible female voice with its scraping yells of evil lust-fulness. Yes, she fills me with horror. And I am stag-gered to find how I believe in her as *the* evil principle. Beelzebub, poor devil, is only one of her instruments.
>
> It is her old, horrible, girning female soul which locks up the heroes, and which sends forth the awful and almost omnipotent malevolence. This old, ghastly woman-spirit is the very core of mischief. And I felt my heart getting as hot against her as the hearts of the lads in the audience were. Red, deep hate I felt of that sym-bolic old ghoul-female. Poor male Beelzebub is her loutish slave. And it takes all Merlin's bright-faced intel-ligence, and all the surging hot urgency of the Paladins, to conquer her.

She will never be finally destroyed—she will never finally die, till her statue, which is immured in the vaults of the castle, is burned. Oh, it was a very psycho-analytic performance altogether, and one could give a very good Freudian analysis of it. But behold this image of the witch: this white, submerged *idea* of woman which rules from the deeps of the unconscious. Behold, the reckless, untamable male knights will do for it. As the statue goes up in flame—it is only paper over wires —the audience yells! And yells again. And would God the symbolic act were really achieved. It is only little boys who yell. Men merely smile at the trick. They know well enough the white image endures. (203)

From feminine Etna to the evil witch of the puppet show, Lawrence returns to his starting point in the plot as he completes his circular journey. He has made no escape from mental consciousness into sensual awareness, nor even into a community of masculine experience. As he leaves the theater, he is buffeted by a shock of intensified loneliness when he shakes hands with his departing companions of the audience. The adventure is over, and his separate personality stands emphasized as the only center of life amidst dreary or vanishing worlds.

The conclusion of *Sea and Sardinia* affirms a strong individual identity far more persuasively than the egoistic declamations of *Aaron's Rod*, but the affirmation is in a melancholy, stoical tone. Though Lawrence preached and pursued the goal of self-realization in individual separateness, he accepted his uniqueness often with misgivings and dread. His aspiration to full psychic liberation and sensual spontaneity was full of dangers, as he of course knew. He understood the necessity of "bitter and wincing realization," but he was nevertheless hampered by his own resistance to the process of self-acknowledgment. He could not, like Walt Whitman, freely throw his arm around the shoulders of his fellowman and walk down the open road, exulting in "the dear love of comrades." One understands his sympathy with fascism or his nostalgia for the emotional richness of the past only as symptoms of his aversion from self-knowledge and responsibility. In glorifying types of suppressions he could lull his fears of full sensual liberty by indulging in a fantasy of bygone life or by subjecting present experience to tyrannical control. Lawrence was affected by these diversionary, ego-protecting impulses all through his creative life, but after the tremendous advance of his art and insight in *Women in Love* the conflict of purposes within him grew more extreme. Near the precipice of a new world of psychic experience—a world that could be sheer horror—he grasped at straws among a swirl of defensive illusions: fascism, subordination of women, adventurous flight, and male errantry. In his work, each time he recovers the courage to face the reality of his inner life, as he does repeatedly, he suffers the heartbreak of disillusionment that is part of the moral crisis and the return to honesty.

Neither his fascist theories nor his nostalgia for the past can withstand the relentless self-analysis of his Introduction to *Memoirs of the Foreign Legion.*[5] Lawrence wrote the essay in January 1922, almost a year after writing *Sea and Sardinia* and six months after finishing *Aaron's Rod.* He re-examines all the events and the feelings of his brief, troublesome relationship with the author, Maurice Magnus: a sponger, defrauder, and a betrayer of men's love who ended his flight from the police by committing suicide in 1920, only months after Lawrence came to know him. Magnus's astonishing treacheries toward all who trusted him fill Lawrence with revulsion, yet he is tormented by the knowledge that he could have saved Magnus's life by giving him more money. He believes that by refusing to aid the man further, after giving several loans that would never be repaid, "I had chosen," Lawrence states, "not to save his life." The essay appraises his responsibility for allowing Magnus to die, and after long, often indirect, deliberations Lawrence reaffirms his spontaneous choice. The essay shows that his determination to let Magnus die issued from a depth of consciousness where the judged and the judge have a common identity, and the ninety-page account of their relations is one of Lawrence's most daring autobiographical pieces—partly because he never mentally recognizes the similarity between their situations in life. He makes only an unconscious, emotional identification.

His characterizations of himself and of Magnus point up the contrasts in their personalities. On the surface, the two men have nothing in common. Magnus was flagrantly extravagant, like an aristocrat expecting others to provide for him whenever he could not give generously to others, while Lawrence was habitually chary with money. His working-man's frugality was well known. Lawrence is cautious, shabby and niggardly next to "the little gentleman" with the lordly social mannerisms, who debases himself in parasitism and swindling in order to keep up appearances. On borrowed money that Magnus accepts as his due he lives at luxury hotels and travels with first-class accommodations, while his bene-factors skimp in their own expenses. He fawns over his patrons, or his favorites, with effusive and womanish attentions that nettle the reticent Lawrence. But Lawrence finds an alertness in Magnus that is attractive, in spite of his repulsive effeminacy and self-abasement. Magnus deserves credit, Lawrence claims, for fighting against the burden of tawdriness that he could not bear in his life, showing always the courage to face his desire and take his risks. "The *human* traitor he was. But he was not traitor to the spirit." (*P2* 359)

When he heard from Magnus soon after their acquaintance in Florence, Lawrence sent five pounds because he discerned an unspoken need in the letter, and he answered to "the strange wistfulness of him appealing to me." Lawrence later visited Magnus because he wanted to see the monastery of Monte Cassino where Magnus was intending to remain as a member of the religious order. This crucial episode in the essay develops from a level of gentle comedy into an expression of intense pathos when Lawrence flees from the place in horror and grief. Magnus greets his guest with a pompous flourish of attentions that is "rather becoming," Lawrence admits, as they meet at the gate of the palatial old fortress of the Church high in the mountains. But, of course, Magnus is deferential to the monks and they are generally curt with him, as with any outsider. Because Lawrence in his usual poverty is thinly dressed for the cold stone monastery in February, Magnus lends him an expensive, black fur-lined coat, and the two sit at dinner with the monks in the icy refectory. Afterwards, conducting Lawrence through the chapels and halls, Magnus who "knew all the short cuts in all the big towns of Europe" delightedly plays cicerone in Monte Cassino: "always in his grey overcoat, and in whispers: me in the big black overcoat, millionairish." Lawrence accepts all the incongruities and discomforts of his first evening with amused, observant irony that is not badly ruffled even when he is trapped into disparaging a glamorous photograph of Magnus's cherished mother.

But the comic tone fades when Lawrence on the next morning is overwhelmed by nostalgia for the past. Looking out Magnus's window, he is moved by the splendor of medievalism, as he was similarly affected by its relics in *Sea and Sardinia*. The pastoral beauty of the place and its romantic spirit have vanished from the modern world. Lawrence gazes yearningly at the farm landscape with its domestic details reminiscent even of the countryside about Eastwood, and to the reader familiar with his recurrent moods, Lawrence once again resembles the adolescent Cyril, narrator of *The White Peacock*, who has such a wistful attitude toward Nethermere. The monastic, rural scene reminds Lawrence of a lost sense of permanence and social unity and passionate experience:

> I looked down on the farm cluster and the brown fields and the sere oak woods of the hill-crown, and the rocks and bushes savagely bordering it round. Beyond, the mountains with their snow were blue-glistery with sunshine, and seemed quite near, but across a sort of gulf. All was still and sunny. And the poignant grip of the past, the grandiose, violent past of the Middle Ages, when blood was strong and unquenched and life was flamboyant with splendours and horrible miseries, took hold of me till I could hardly bear it. It was really agony to me to be in the monastery and to see the old farm and the bullocks slowly working in the fields below, and the black pigs rooting among weeds, and to see a monk sitting on a parapet in the sun, and an old, old man in skin sandals and white bunched, swathed legs come driving an ass slowly to the monastery gate, slowly, with all that lingering nonchalance and wildness of the Middle Ages, and yet to know that I was myself, child of the present. It was so strange from M—'s window to look down on the plain and see the white road going straight past a mountain that stood like a loaf of sugar, the river meandering in loops, and the railway with glistening lines making a long black sweep across the flat and into the hills. To see the station like a little harbour where

trucks like shipping stood anchored in rows in the black
bay of railway. To see trains stop in the station and tiny
people swarming like flies! To see all this from the monastery, where the Middle Ages live on in a sort of
agony, like Tithonus, and cannot die, this was almost a
violation to my soul, made almost a wound. (*P2* 318–19)

The industrialism of the present day, viewed from the
mountain in the reduced perspective of the valley, is emblematic of our diminished humanity, and in a surge of revulsion Lawrence would withdraw from it to embrace the
memorials of a more expressive way of life. But in his continuing exposure to the symbols of the past, he finds a greater horror in the blindly persisting, soul-destroyed anachronisms
"that cannot die." As he and Magnus walk along the slope of
the hill Lawrence sees in an old-world peasant the inhuman
will-to-live that sustains even crows and lizards, "having no
idea and no sustained emotion," but compelled by insentient,
strong blood to keep on with the eternal round of sameness.
Granted, he would choose the company of the peasant before
he chose a life in the company of Magnus, but only because
the peasant lacks Magnus's "readiness to rush into speech,
and . . . the exhaustive nature of his presence." Wearied as
he is by febrile, mechanistic modernity, Lawrence senses that
his feeling about the monastery contains a wish to regress toward a fatal attraction:

> We were seated, in the sunny afternoon, on the wild
> hill-top high above the world. Across the stretch of pale,
> dry, standing thistles that peopled the waste ground, and
> beyond the rocks was the ruined convent. Rocks rose
> behind us, the summit. Away on the left were the
> woods which hid us from the great monastery. This was
> the mountain top, the last foothold of the old world.
> Below we could see the plain, the straight white road,

straight as a thought, and the more flexible black railway
with the railway station. There swarmed the *ferrovieri*
like ants. There was democracy, industrialism, socialism,
the red flag of the communists and the red, white and
green tricolor of the fascisti. That was another world.
And how bitter, how barren a world! Barren like the
black cinder-track of the railway, with its two steel
lines.

And here above, sitting with the little stretch of pale,
dry thistles around us, our back to a warm rock, we
were in the Middle Ages. Both worlds were agony to
me. But here, on the mountain top was worst: The past,
the poignancy of the not-quite-dead past.

"I think one's got to go through with the life down
there—get somewhere beyond it. One can't go back," I
said to him. (*P2* 324–25)

The glamor of the past is such a strange burden on his feelings that Lawrence is miserable as he walks with Magnus
away from the hilltop:

I feeling as if my heart had once more broken: I don't
know why. And he feeling his fear of life, that haunted
him, and his fear of his own self and its consequences,
that never left him for long. And he seemed to walk
close to me, very close. And we had neither of us anything more to say. (*P2* 326)

In this passage, Lawrence painfully frees himself from the
attractive illusion that Magnus and the monastic institution
uphold. The ancient order is especially appealing to Lawrence
as an example of the brotherhood he seeks, a community of
men devoted to an exalted ideal. But the disturbing figure of
the subhuman peasant, whose soul was never formed because
of the burdens of old-world and rural deprivations, provided
the reminder to Lawrence that social order—even monastic
brotherhood—is apt to be maintained by pithing individual

life. Lawrence escapes his spell of yearning for the alleged emotional richness and unity of experience in the past. Recognizing the sterility of the barren rock and dry thistles, the ruined convent, and the wealthy monks' haughty withdrawal from the common world of men, Lawrence rejects his earlier romantic notion that on this hilltop he found "that lingering nonchalance and wildness of the Middle Ages." He explains Magnus's nostalgia for an imaginary perfection of life by noting that Magnus lived in "fear of his own self and its consequences." Without explicitly judging himself, Lawrence acknowledges his similar fear by being uneasily conscious that Magnus assumes safety with him, and that Magnus "seemed to walk close to me, very close." Deprived of the comforting fancy that love and unity survive in the medieval design of life, Lawrence decides to leave Monte Cassino directly, and he departs still feeling oppressed by its ambiguous beauty and mocking hopelessness. Back among the cities of the coast, he sits like one torn away from all that had once appeared desirable:

> There on the steamer I sat in a bit of sunshine, and felt that again the world had come to an end for me, and again my heart was broken. The steamer seemed to be making its way away from the old world, that had come to another end in me. (*P2* 328)

Accepting responsibility for himself, as Magnus would not do, Lawrence is disenchanted by any alternatives to the world of commerce and nationalism that appeared repulsive from the mountaintop. The hope of love and unity prevailing in the contemporary industrial system seems bitterly impossible. Mass wars are fought in the modern world, and men—like Magnus—vilely exploit one another even in friendships. Lawrence's distress over men's aggressions rises to the edge of hys-

teria following his descent from the mountain, as he denounces the sophisticated weaponry that gives effect to a
pure, abstract lust to kill. The real world to which Lawrence
sadly returns affords him no "eternal union with a man," but,
instead, strife and consciousness of solitude in his effort to establish his relationships to the people and the world around
him. For this decisive moment, Lawrence recognizes that his
nostalgic dream of perfect life is fed by his excessive fear of
man's aggression, the "fear of his own self and its consequences," that he identified in Magnus. Wrestling with his
fear, he rages against warfare to say that he can triumph morally over the worst that man can do; and then, gradually
quietening, he resumes consideration of his responsibility for
letting Magnus die—which is what threatens to shame Lawrence as the worst that he had done.

When Magnus turns up at Fontana Vecchia as a fugitive
from Italy, crying out that " 'A terrible thing has happened,' " Lawrence greets him "rather unwillingly, because I
detest terrible things, and the people to whom they happen."
(*P2* 329) It is clear to him that Magnus will re-create his
doom however his opportunities for life may outwardly
change. But he gives him more money and writes more letters
on his behalf, until he is sick of the whole effort to keep Magnus going. Lawrence in the persona of Rawdon Lilly thought
that he wanted soul-submission from lesser beings; but Lawrence in his actual life could never brook submission from another person. In practice, if not always in theory, he remained
the same soul's-democrat who forbore to ask Frieda to remain
with him at Lake Garda because she had to acknowledge responsibility for her choice. Magnus had to be responsible for
his desire also, even if it led him into death.

Magnus becomes heroic, finally, for following the promptings of his own soul: "In the great spirit of human consciousness he was a hero, little, quaking and heroic: a strange, quaking little star." (*P2* 359) In the elegiac conclusion to the essay Lawrence is humanely conscious of the conflicting loyalties that one owes to oneself and also to men who have given their trust, for that trust creates the one fragile community of souls in this world:

> *Also—M—! Ich grüsse dich, in der Ewigkeit. Aber*
> *heir, im Herzblut, hast du Gift und Leid nachgelassen—*
> to use your own romantic language. (*P2* 361)

Less intense than Birkin's final scene in *Women in Love*, and more bitter than the ending of *Sea and Sardinia*, this conclusion nevertheless expresses Lawrence's similar grief over the catastrophe of human relationships. Gerald and Magnus both illustrate the doom that man carries in his own heart, and Birkin and Lawrence grieve for their lost assurances that men can give courage to one another through generous, manly love. Lawrence's separate identity is again underscored, as it was in *Sea and Sardinia*, but clearly the accumulating venom and sorrow left in his heart have weakened him.

In spite of the decision he made on Monte Cassino two years earlier—"to go through with the life down there"— Lawrence could not easily continue his involvements with humanity. While he was writing the Introduction, he was deliberating alternatives in his immediate life between a withdrawal into quietism or further, purposive activity in the world. For a few months he had invitations in hand that forced him, or seemed so to Lawrence, to make such a fateful choice. The alternatives pitched him into dizzying vacillation that came to a peak in January 1922 while he was reexamining the meaning of his experience with Magnus.

From Taos, New Mexico, Lawrence received an invitation to be the guest of Mabel Dodge Sterne. She had read *Sea and Sardinia*, or at least its opening chapters,[6] and she wanted its author to write something equally marvelous about Taos. Her repeated invitations offered Lawrence the wealthy literary sponsor in the United States that Amy Lowell had earlier refused to become. He now had a clear opportunity to pursue his lingering resolution "to transfer all my life to America." But his friends Earl and Achsah Brewster, American Buddhists whom he had met on Capri, were also inviting him to come to Ceylon, where they were giving up the world. Brewster thought that Buddhism would bring Lawrence peace.[7]

Lawrence did not know for certain just how he felt even about peace. His initial response to Brewster's proselytizing was a flamboyant, archly romantic rejection of any philosophy of self-effacement:

> If you kill all tigers still the tiger-soul continues. The mankind which kills the tiger assumes, willy-nilly, the tiger's nature and need of being.—Just as white America assumes, inevitably and frighteningly, the Red Indian nature—little by little.—But the point is, I don't *want* the tiger superseded. Oh, may each she-tigress have seventy-seven whelps, and may they all grow in strength and shine in stripes like day and night, and may each one eat at least seventy miserable featherless human birds, and lick red chops of gusto after it. Leave me my tigers, leave me spangled leopards, leave me bright cobra snakes, and I wish I had poison fangs and talons as good. I *believe* in wrath and gnashing of teeth and crunching of cowards' bones. I *believe* in fear and in pain and in oh, such a lot of sorrow. As for your white Nirvana, my boy: paint stripes on it, and see how it looks. I'll bet it has a tiger's hungry sides and buzzing, disagreeable tail.

Only it's like Well's [sic] Invisible Man, it makes no
show except when it's had its dinner. (*CL* 651–52)

When he could sustain this attitude even in a milder, more
reflective mood, he felt determined to go to America, and he
would write to Brewster that "the East is not my destiny":

> More and more I feel that meditation and the inner life
> are not my aim, but some sort of action and strenuous-
> ness and pain and frustration and struggling through. All
> the things you don't believe in I do. . . .
> I have decided to go to Taos in New Mexico. There
> are Indians there, and an old sun-magic—And I believe
> that the clamorous future is in the States. I do not want
> peace nor beauty nor even freedom from pain. I want to
> fight and to feel new gods in the flesh. (*CL* 681)

But two weeks later he was wavering again, and he wanted
to change his mind:

> For the first time, I suddenly feel you may be right and
> I wrong: that I am kicking against the pricks. I have
> misinterpreted "Life is sorrow." . . .
> I believe you are right. Probably there, east, is the
> *source:* and America is the extreme periphery. Oh God,
> must one go to the extreme limit, then to come back?
> I only know it seems so much *easier*, more peaceful to
> come east. But then peace, peace! I am *so* mistrustful of
> it: so much afraid that it means a sort of weakness and
> giving in. Yet I believe you're right. The very word you
> say, that Ceylon is *heavy*, makes me think you are right.
> And the fact that I have felt so *spiteful* against
> Buddha makes me feel I was unsure all the time, and
> kicking against the pricks.
> We have made all arrangements to go to Taos, New
> Mexico. But we have booked no passage. Shall I come to
> Ceylon? *Dio mio*, I am so ridiculous, wavering between
> East and West.
> I believe I shall not go to America. (*CL* 685)

Lawrence did not elect the alternative that he stoically, implicitly chooses in his Introduction to the *Memoirs*. Instead, he went to Ceylon. But he hardly experienced it at all; he fell ill and wrote nothing. Four weeks after his arrival, he embarked for Australia. Australia, surely, was the newest world of all, where one could make a life of strenuous, significant activity. A largely unformed nation, extremely democratic and socially fluid, it might be the proper seedbed for a new idea, a new bond among men.

But in *Kangaroo* Lawrence cannot take social earnestness seriously, not even his own. He implies that his persona is something of a fool for his misdirected involvement with social questions: "Poor Richard Lovatt wearied himself to death struggling with the problem of himself, and calling it Australia." Richard Lovatt Somers is an English writer—"a comical looking bloke!" as he appears to lounging Australian workmen—who arrives in "this new country, the youngest country on the globe, to start a new life and flutter with a new hope." (I) But he frets over the apparent vacuity of "accomplished liberty," and he resents the egalitarian manners of the Australians. His domestic life among neighbors and his opportunities for comradeship suggest his boyhood in the rural Midlands, and that makes him "vaguely depressed":

> The pleasant heartiness of the life he had known as a boy now depressed him. He hated the promiscuous mixing in of all the company, the lack of reserve in manner. He had preferred India for that: the gulf between the native servants and the whites kept up a sort of tone. He had learned to be separate, to talk across a slight distance. And that was an immense relief to him, because it was really more his nature. Now he found himself soused again in the old familiar "jolly and cosy" spirit of his childhood and boyhood, and he was depressed. (II)

The novel is a joyless, often sardonic comedy about everyone's futile cross-purposes. As soon as he settles in suburban
Sydney, Somers longs to be back in Europe. "Oh, God, to be
in Europe, lovely, lovely Europe that he had hated so thoroughly and abused so vehemently, saying it was moribund
and stale and finished. The fool was himself." As soon as he is
ready to leave Australia he is torn by love for its delicate
beauty, and he considers remaining there for ever. In the central plot, Lawrence puts Somers into contacts with organized
socialists and organized fascists and Somers turns away in dis-
gust from the destructiveness of both parties. The excerpts of
newspaper reportage that Lawrence accumulates in a chapter
called "Bits" are another indication to Somers that society
does not correspond to any coherent feelings or ideas he once
had about life:

> Bits, bits, bits. Yet Richard Lovatt read on. It was not
> mere anecdotage. It was the momentaneous life of the
> continent. There was no consecutive thread. Only the
> laconic courage of experience.
> All the better. He could have kicked himself for
> wanting to help mankind, join in revolutions or reforms
> or any of that stuff. And he kicked himself still harder
> thinking of his frantic struggles with the "soul" and the
> "dark god" and the "listeners" and the "answerer."
> Blarney—blarney—blarney! He was a preacher and a
> blatherer, and he hated himself for it. Damn the "soul,"
> damn the "dark god," damn the "listener" and the "an-
> swerer," and above all, damn his own interfering, nosy
> self. (XIV)

The "consecutive thread" of the novel is also not very
strong. The novel easily turns from the plot into digressions
that are more interesting than the central narrative. They are
unified thematically as further illustrations of the variances

and conflicts that muddle every effort, but the best ones have little to do with the story or the pretense of fictional characters. "Harriet and Lovatt at Sea in Marriage" is a chapter of rather brittle hilarity about the state of Lawrence's own marriage. He analyzes the alternatives for the future when lovers marry and discover that "two fierce and opposing currents meet in the narrows of perfect-love." Lawrence recommends that a wise wife should let the ship drift into the calm Pacific ocean of male lordship and masterdom, even if she must laugh up her sleeve at the self-important captain. But most women prefer, as Harriet does, to steer their marriage into the gray "democratic Atlantic of *perfect* companionship" between friends and equals. In a spirited little allegory, Lovatt sews a new flag with a phoenix on it and he wants to rechristen the ship; Harriet squashes his intention with withering ridicule that wins the reader to her side. Instead of a natural master, Lovatt indeed appears to be:

> the most forlorn and isolated creature in the world, without even a dog to his command. He was so isolated he was hardly a man at all, among men. He had absolutely nothing but her. Among men he was like some unbelievable creature, an emu for example. Like an emu in the streets or in a railway carriage. He might well say phoenix. (IX)

The other memorable digression is Lawrence's chapter on "The Nightmare" (XII) of his war years in England. His recollection of his sickening disillusionment with a supposedly enlightened society, his insight to the abasement of all men in wartime, and his account of frustration and harassment in the hands of a suspicious officialdom: all this is so vividly registered that no essay equals it for the analysis of war's effect on a sensitive civilian's consciousness. Lawrence's pain over his brutalization and the occasional straining of his voice in hyperbolic denunciations record the subtle terrors that were a shrill tone in his life during the war.

Lawrence cannot make Australia personally relevant in a way that could hold him there or even sustain his novel. Somers comes to love the landscape "that was so clear and clean, clean of all fogginess or confusion"; and he recognizes that the nation "is the land that as yet has made no great mistake, humanly. The horrible human mistakes of Europe. And probably, the even worse human mistakes of America." But the absence of any welter of moral definition leaves the place meaningless to him, and he departs for San Francisco. " 'You have got to go *through* the mistakes,' " he explains to himself. (XVIII)

At last won over by Mabel Dodge's urging, Lawrence arrived in America in September 1922. Immediately he set to work writing about the Southwestern desert and the New Mexico Indians, and during the three years he lived in the United States he never attempted a serious imaginative account of the rest of the country in its urban, modern aspects. He traveled in other parts of the country, visited many of the major cities, and he had opportunities to write about a fuller range of American civilization than he chose to examine. Not even the evidence of advanced industrialism and its cultural effects were of any real interest to him. Most of the United States merely annoyed him. He was especially disposed to ridicule the American tourists and bohemian artists who take up a shallow interest in their "wild west." In a style marked by whimsy and mockery, Lawrence dismisses all that seems self-consciously contrived in the Southwest. He is piqued by the "comic-opera" spectacle out in a desert where all the participants play their roles with farcical solemnity. Anyone's expe-

rience seems only another "stunt" amidst the incongruities of
rich tourists, local artists, ecstatic highbrow curiosity seek-
ers, macabre Mexicans, and ghost-like Indians wound in sheets
"like Hamlet's father's ghost, with a lurking smile":

> And here am I, a lone lorn Englishman, tumbled out
> of the known world of the British Empire onto this
> stage: for it persists in seeming like a stage to me, and
> not like the proper world. (*P* 92)

But when he writes about the landscape and its Indians as
symbols of the features of the soul, irony and impatience fall
away from him. He does not frolic with the material or twit
the reader; he does not use himself or his subject or his language cheaply when he is under the spell of aboriginal America. His two styles, by clearly discriminating between what is
meaningful to him and what is trivial in the United States, indicate the direction that Lawrence's art and personal quest
will continue to take in America. Precisely descriptive of the
stark desert world, his Southwestern writings also record
his worsening isolation and his increasing self-absorption as he
comes into daily contact with obscurely personal, symbolic
facts in the landscape around him and tries to realize their
meaning.

The pueblo of Taos immediately struck Lawrence with its
aura of finality, "like one of the old monasteries of Europe."
Lawrence wrote in the *Dial* that the Taos pueblo is the nodality of an ancient way of life that survives diminished and helpless, preserving a quality of experience that must not be lost
from consciousness. His brief, initial impression of the place is
anecdotal except when a revulsion and a sense of doom steal
over him, as they did at Monte Cassino, when he feels the grip
of the past:

There it is, then, the pueblo, as it has been since heaven knows when. And the slow dark weaving of the Indian life going on still, though perhaps more waveringly. And oneself, sitting there on a pony, a far-off stranger with gulfs of time between me and this. And yet, the old nodality of the pueblo still holding, like a dark ganglion spinning invisible threads of consciousness. A sense of dryness, almost of weariness, about the pueblo. And a sense of the inalterable. It brings a sick sort of feeling over me, always, to get into the Indian vibration. Like breathing chlorine. (*P* 101)

Lawrence's momentary, ambivalent involvement in the scene is typified in the figure of himself on horseback, distantly observing the age-old reality that compels his sympathy. A similar perspective and emotion are more artfully sustained in another essay for *Dial* when Lawrence writes about his first contact with Indians. Mabel Dodge took him to an Apache tribal gathering soon after his arrival, and his account is filled with detailed description of the event. But his own sensibility becomes the explicit topic of attention in the essay, as he inquires why "an acute sadness, and a nostalgia, unbearably yearning for something, and a sickness of the soul came over me."

He portrays himself walking about the encampment, discovering the hypnotic chants and dance-steps of the Indian rituals; he notices the full petticoats of the dark-skirted women and the black steeple hats worn by the men who adopt Western dress, while others are in cotton flannel sheets; he notices the thin-tailed dogs that trail after the tilted wagons; and everywhere there is the burning sulphurous smell of the Apache camp. At night small campfires flicker on the side of the low hill. With a blanket drawn close about him for the cold, he wanders near to the ring of chanters who are gathered around a tribal fire. There, he finds what a "proper world" should have: the unconscious bond among men and the common sympathies that are evident in the familial order of tribal life. Because of its communality, the primitive scene has great power over his emotions even as he accepts responsibility for carrying his bit of consciousness into freer, wider relations in a world of his own. In this essay, as at the conclusion of *Sea and Sardinia*, Lawrence remains a solitary figure making his own way despite his vague yearning for communal experience. Just as he could not join the Sicilians who come repeatedly to the puppet show, he cannot become a primitive being and sit around a campfire listening to tribal chants:

> The soul is as old as the oldest day, and has its own hushed echoes, its own far-off tribal understandings sunk and incorporated. We do not need to live the past over again. Our darkest tissues are twisted in this old tribal experience, our warmest blood came out of the old tribal fire. And they vibrate still in answer, our blood, our tissue. But me, the conscious me, I have gone a long road since then. And as I look back, like memory terrible as bloodshed, the dark faces round the fire in the night, and one blood beating in me and them. But I don't want to go back to them, ah, never. I never want to deny them or break with them. But there is no going back. Always onward, still further. The great devious onward-flowing stream of conscious human blood. From them to me, and from me on.
>
> I don't want to live again the tribal mysteries my blood has lived long since. I don't want to know as I have known, in the tribal exclusiveness. But every drop of me trembles still alive to the old sound, every thread in my body quivers to the frenzy of the old mystery. I know my derivation. I was born of no virgin, of no Holy Ghost. Ah, no, these old men telling the tribal tale

were my fathers. I have a dark-faced, bronze-voiced father far back in the resinous ages. My mother was no
virgin. She lay in her hour with this dusky-lipped tribe-
father. And I have not forgotten him. But he, like many
an old father with a changeling son, he would like to
deny me. But I stand on the far edge of their firelight,
and am neither denied nor accepted. My way is my
own, old red father; I can't cluster at the drum any
more. (P 98–99)

The reaffirmation of individuated, independent character is
a familiar structural pattern in Lawrence's works, but an interesting anomaly in this essay is that his idiom changes at the
very peak of his resolve. After a beautifully sustained evoca-
tion of the Indian ethos and his sympathetic detachment from
it as a modern man, Lawrence's last paragraph unexpectedly
links his acknowledgment of the "tribal mysteries" to his
acknowledgment of an exclusive sexual relation between par-
ental figures. In dramatizing his actual detachment from
Indian life his rhetoric passes, or slips, into admitting that the
basis of family organization, the conjugal relation, had previously also excluded him. It is the parallel between his adult
social alienation and the pain of his childhood family experience that explains, in this essay and in his preceding travel
writings as well, why Lawrence falls into such distress at each
"pungent awakening to the lost past." His separation from the
anachronistic tribal community—as from the monastic brotherhood, and the Sicilian fellowship—revives the bitterness of
his exclusion from the conjugal community of his parents:
"the past that cannot die."

In his first encounters with the New Mexico landscape
Lawrence found continuing evidence of his separation from
other human beings. The context of desert isolation lent itself
to recalling the primary alienation in his life, and the old grief

of love for his mother rose once more to explicit expression. Within two months after his arrival in Taos he wrote a poem of yearning for reunion with his dead mother, whom he had not written about for seven years. In "Spirits Summoned West" (*CP* 410–12) Lawrence entreats his mother to come join him in the Rocky Mountains now that she is free of her husband and the burden of mortality. His heart is the proper, long-prepared home for her unfulfilled virgin soul which only he saw and loved in her:

> Come back then, mother, my love, whom I told to die.
> It was only I who saw the virgin you
> That had no home.
>
> The overlooked virgin,
> My love.
>
> You overlooked her too.
>
> Now that the grave is made of mother and wife,
> Now that the grave is made and lidded over with turf:
>
> *Come, delicate, overlooked virgin, come back to me*
> *And be still,*
> *Be glad.*
>
> I didn't tell you to die, for nothing.
> I wanted the virgin you to be home at last
> In my heart.
>
> Inside my innermost heart,
> Where the virgin in woman comes home to a man.
>
> The homeless virgin
> Who never in all her life could find the way home
> To that difficult innermost place in a man.

Aesthetically, this poem is of small interest, except for Lawrence's use of a Whitman form in the sentence-stanzas and the alternation of voices between the recitative and aria strains.

The poem underscores a biographical point, however. Lawrence's attitude toward his past remained as ambivalent as it had been years earlier, and the ambivalence has come to be confused with and reflected by his response to western America. The tone and argument of the poem directly conflict with the stoical conclusion to the Apache essay. From one moment to the next, Lawrence represents his mother as a pathetically doomed virgin and as a teeming squaw. In the same passages the father-figure is an insensitive husband or a proud, commanding brave. And the common ground of intense feeling in both passages is the author's anxiety over his state of separation and singleness.

Whether as symptom or as cause, the emotional stress evident in the work of this period indicates the significance of Lawrence's self-dramatizing techniques. Alone in a contemporary world that is largely lost to him, as the past also felt lost to him, his own figure becomes a center of arbitrary authority. He presents his clearly identified persona as the only image of a viable morality and a life-bearing consciousness amidst an environment that is anachronistic, exclusive, and symbolic of some agony in himself. This recurrent figuration expresses his sense of living "in a world of perilous, pure freedom, having always the tincture of fear, danger, and exultance." When he felt exultant over his freedom, he equated it with true democracy, as in his essay on Cooper, where the phrase appears. When he felt fearful about freedom, he disparaged "the vacuity of accomplished liberty," as he again spoke of democracy after he approached it in Australia. His political viewpoints are mainly metaphors for the direction of his unconscious aspiration toward self-recognition or toward self-denial. For Lawrence, solitary freedom was the threshold of dangerous, fateful action—as it was for Gerald Crich when

Birkin and Ursula withdrew from the Alpine setting—and he was too wise to accept that state with simple anticipation.

Lawrence fully exploited the self-dramatizing method when he rewrote the literary essays that finally appeared in book form as *Studies in Classic American Literature*. When he first composed the essays his motive was to give rational coherence to his "whole *Weltanschauung*," and he jealously guarded his work from presumed plagiarists who would misunderstand its meaning. But during the winter of 1922–23 he entirely recast the earlier version and unhesitatingly changed the character of his work, adding passages, deleting others, reshaping or rephrasing the entire text. Major ideas over which he labored at length in version 1 now dwindled in importance or disappeared from his work. He does not give extended explanations of the historical and biopsychic theories that underlie his criticism. In the first chapter, still entitled "The Spirit of Place," he omits most of the discussion of geography and history, and the remaining references to the spirit of place are not fully intelligible. In place of the former historical analysis of American culture, Lawrence denounces the subjugation of the individual in a democratic society; Armin Arnold observed that in its final form the chapter might better be called "Democracy and Slavery." [8] Lawrence railed against the social liberty that caricatured his own venture toward independence.

Throughout the volume he presents very little argument to the logical point of view. Instead of addressing himself, as he did earlier, to the intellectual imagination with theories, symbols, and a vast intricacy of related ideas, he presents his material in a popular, flippant style. He introduced a wealth of deliberately ludicrous images, Western diction, journalistic typography, and in general he disrupted the restrained reflectiveness of the earlier studies. American slang explodes across nearly every page, and the audacity of his idiom draws attention to himself. Lawrence is very much to the fore in *Classic American Literature*, dramatizing his own volatile personality as an antidote to the "mechanical contrivance" of American identity. In version 1 Lawrence had criticized Franklin, for instance, by sober logical refutation; but in version 3 he creates new standards of value and imposes judgments by force of his intense, spontaneous response alone. He exposes Franklin with a series of satirical exclamations; he negates his creed by offering a creed of his own that is melodramatically mystical and belligerently enigmatic; and he supplants Franklin's famous list of virtues with an iconoclastic list of his own, including: "CLEANLINESS: Don't be too clean. It impoverishes the blood." In contrast to Franklin, the reasonable democratic slave who cares most for what is common among men, Lawrence flaunts his idiosyncratic, unqualifiable uniqueness:

> Oh Benjamin! Oh Binjum! You do NOT suck me in any longer.
> And why oh why should the snuff-colored little trap have wanted to take us all in? Why did he do it?
> Out of sheer human cussedness, in the first place. We do all like to get things inside a barbed-wire corral. Especially our fellow-men. We love to round them up inside the barbed-wire enclosure of FREEDOM, and make 'em work. "*Work, you free jewel, WORK!*" shouts the liberator, cracking his whip. Benjamin, I will not work. I do not choose to be a free democrat. I am absolutely a servant of my own Holy Ghost.

The book has its passages of restrained exposition and moving eloquence, most of which were adapted from version 1, but the rhetoric which leaves its impression in the mind of the reader is Lawrence's humorously derisive histrionics. Sometimes he is outrageously funny, as in his description of Poe's style and in his caricatures of Whitman.

Throughout the spring and summer of 1923 he continued to write in the same unnervingly comical vein that relies on purposely ludicrous images and extravagant irony. In reviewing Stuart Sherman's book on eminent Americans, Lawrence uses the method to mock sentimentalities and equivocations in the professor's work:

> Well there is Professor Sherman's dish of cookies which he bids you eat and have. An awfully sweet book, all about having your cookies and eating 'em. The cookies are Tradition, and Heroes, and Great Men, and $350,000,000 in your pocket. And eating 'em is Democracy, Serving Mankind, piously giving most of the $350,000,000 back again. "Oh, nobly and heroically get $350,000,000 together," chants Professor Sherman in this litany of having your cookies and eating 'em, "and then piously and munificently give away $349,000,000 again." (P 320–21)

In reviewing an anthology of current American verse he quotes a few obviously bad poems and makes telling satirical remarks about them:

> Old soup of old bones of life, heated up again for a new consommé. Nearly always called printanière.
>> *I know a forest, stilly deep. . .*
> Mark the poetic novelty of stilly-deep, and then say there is nothing new under the sun.
>> *My soul-harp never thrills to peaceful tunes:*
> I should say so.
>>> *For after all, the thing to do*
>>> *Is just to put your heart in song—*
> Or in pickle. (P 326)

In discussing contemporary fiction in an article titled "Surgery for the Novel—or A Bomb," Lawrence chiefly mimics the self-conscious sensibility that modern novels analyze and he ridicules the literary achievement of Joyce and Proust:

> So there you have the "serious" novel, dying in a very long-drawn-out fourteen-volume death-agony, and absorbedly, childishly interested in the phenomenon. "Did I feel a twinge in my little toe, or didn't I?" asks every character of Mr. Joyce or of Miss Richardson or M. Proust. Is my aura a blend of frankincense and orange pekoe and boot-blacking, or is it myrrh and bacon-fat and Shetland tweed? The audience round the death-bed gapes for the answer. And when, in a sepulchral tone, the answer comes at length, after hundreds of pages: "It is none of these, it is abysmal chloro-coryambasis," the audience quivers all over, and murmurs: "That's just how I feel myself." (P 517)

When he went to Mexico later in the summer, he began a series of anti-Christian essays which are written in the same flamboyant manner. All his writing in America that is not directly descriptive of nature and Indian life bristles with sardonic impatience over the inadequacy of discursive, verbal communication of ideas. He was writing mainly to shock, to unsettle, to attack the minds of other people. But in making forays at "pot-bound" American consciousness, Lawrence was not writing in a way that was revelatory or commanding to himself. He had removed his deepest feelings from his work by pursuing that theatrical style which devalues all outward, common experience, including his own observations as a traveler and critic of life and literature.

But Lawrence never spoiled his symbolic language with any superficiality or irreverence in his descriptions of nature and the details of aboriginal culture. The sharp division in his writing styles is a sign of the division of sensibility that left his profounder self silent and utterly detached from the contemporary social world by which he had earlier approached "the problem of himself." Lawrence came to a point of extreme solitary stress that must have appeared to him as a cul de sac. Unable yet to "go *through* with" the next struggle of self-realization, he grew more noticeably impatient with the external, human world that he had largely dismissed in his art. Numerous accounts of his first year around Taos and in Mexico, however inaccurate or biased they may be about the details or meaning of any single incident, all take note of Lawrence's unusually high-strung nerves and uncontrollable outbursts,[9] and Lawrence himself acknowledges his special irritableness in America.[10]

This state of mind in Lawrence may well have provoked the domestic catastrophe of a separation from Frieda which, for a while, seemed likely to be final. In Mexico, Frieda insisted upon their returning to England, presumably to reside there permanently. Murry was at this moment also begging Lawrence to return and join him in another magazine venture. Lawrence wavered in partial agreement—he would go back for a visit—but after accompanying Frieda to New York where they booked passage, they again disagreed and this time he decided to remain alone in America. Frieda indignantly sailed for London and Lawrence traveled back westward by train. He stopped to see acquaintances in Buffalo and in Chicago before rejoining two young Danish painters in Los Angeles whom the Lawrences had known at Kiowa ranch the winter before. Lawrence talked of the three men going to sea on a merchant ship, or of founding a utopian colony in Mexico. Fatuously, he once accompanied them to a young peoples' dance, where a flapper called him Santa Claus because of his beard. Overwrought and disconsolate, he undertook a strenuous train and mule-back journey from Los Angeles back to central Mexico, this time accompanied by one of the painters, who reported in letters to the other that Lawrence seemed at times to be "really insane":

> Lawrence is a queer snail, and impossible to under-stand. He seems to be absolutely nuts at times, and to have a hard time with himself. He thinks he can show by his feelings what people think and do. At other times he is so reasonable and so overwhelmingly good that there is no end to it. . . . He makes everything much more artificial and complicated than it is in reality. He is afraid Frieda will avoid him; he says that she can have a house in London and have her children with her, then he can travel alone. "She will hate it before long," he says, biting his lower lip and nodding small, quick nods. Do you know him? The fact is that he is afraid she will like that arrangement only too well.[11]

By the winter of 1923 Lawrence's life was totally disrupted as it had not been since the death of his mother. The impossi-bility of continuing in such emotional chaos led him, at last, to return to England in December for a reconciliation with Frieda. But the situation which he found there, whether or not he learned its exact details, only further complicated his psychological peril. Upon Frieda's return to London she had immediately won the sympathy of Murry, whose wife had recently died. When Frieda visited her family in Germany, Murry accompanied her to the Continent, and there she pro-posed that they have an affair. He wrestled with his con-science and refused her, only because, he believed, it would have been disloyal to Lawrence.[12] When Lawrence arrived on the scene in London, it is likely that he acquired some in-tuition of what had happened. In a tense, drunken episode at a "Last Supper" in the Café Royal—a place truly jinxed for Lawrence [13]—the word *betrayal*, heavy with both its biblical and sexual references, passed designedly between the two

men. Mrs. Carswell, who was at the dinner, makes it clear by
her bias against Murry and Frieda that as a witness even she
sensed or knew the implications of the *betrayal*.[14] Lawrence
could not have been entirely unknowing. The rancor with
which he lampooned Murry in four short stories during the
following few months shows Lawrence's bitterness against his
former blood-brother.[15]

These private details of his life are important to note because Lawrence's present circumstances bizarrely produced in
real life the fantasy-situation plaguing his unconscious. Just
when he felt most isolated, his wife left him and offered herself to the one man to whom Lawrence looked for the manly
love that would, in his eyes, confirm his masculinity. If Lawrence had previously seen in Murry a soul's brother and a potential lover, Murry's role was now stripped nakedly to the
figure of a sexually enviable, threatening father. The love
from a man that Lawrence badly needed was once again denied him because of rivalry over a woman. Murry's transformation from symbolic brother-lover to father-aggressor dangerously externalized Lawrence's fear of men which underlay
his homoerotic desires. Perilously at the edge of a breakdown,
Lawrence was pushed farther toward effeminacy as the only
way to win manly love—and deeper into defensive hatred of
the male power that attracted him.

Under such an urgent pyschological burden, it is significant
that Lawrence was anxious to get back to New Mexico. A return to America was perhaps the most practical way to re-
establish his marriage; it was also a return to the richly symbolic natural world of the Southwest where he felt that he
could discover the compelling motives of his unconscious
life.

6

"The inner chaos
of the Rockies"

After returning to Kiowa ranch with Frieda, and accompanied by Dorothy Brett,[1] Lawrence worked without distracting interruptions or any stinting throughout the summer and fall of 1924. In a series of related stories and descriptive essays he closely examined the surrounding landscape and the symbol that the place was to him. Thus intensively explored, his America proved to be no seed-ground for a utopia, nor did it support his hope for a new world of psychic freedom. The Southwestern locale in Lawrence's work comes to represent chaos in nature, and Lawrence suffered a severe life-crisis as he recognized the chaos of his innermost self. Trying to get at the symbolic meaning of the landscape, he momentarily regained an intenser, more analytic vision of life than any he had written since completing *Women in Love*. But he achieved it only by abandoning the level of realism that he had maintained in his earlier fictions. The plausible, familiar world of the Morels and Brangwens, or even the Sissons, the Somerses or the Lawrences themselves, is superseded by an alien world that includes ghosts, satyrs, gnomish wizards, spellbound, nameless women, lost Indian tribes, sacred mountains and lakes, and a fraternity of costumed Mexicans presuming to be gods. His recourse to fantasy figures, especially those of witchcraft, suggests the nightmarish quality of his new vision which was sporadic and extremely ambiguous. Lawrence never fully expressed his new insight in one unified major work. Fitfully, and often with violence to the piece of fiction at hand, he approached an intense awareness of himself during his second sojourn in America, from which he recoiled in aversion while he completed *The Plumed Serpent*. At that moment, in Mexico, he suffered a tubercular attack that kept him chronically ill until his death five years later. The literary evidence indicates that under the stress of his painful self-explorations he also suffered an emotional collapse in America from which his art, like his health, never fully recovered.[2]

Lawrence's writings during this period of his crisis reveal attitudes of sexual ambivalence that differ sharply from those expressed in his earlier works. Instead of his usual distress over the sensual weakness of male characters who are dominated by aggressive women, Lawrence displays a fascinated horror as overpowered female characters surrender themselves to sexually virulent males. All three of the stories he wrote during the summer in New Mexico are about women with an evil spell over their lives who deliver themselves to erotic destruction in the mountains of western America. Half-approving what he fearfully brings into focus out of his subconscious, the author shows a willingness to rationalize or glorify what he abhors as viciousness and brutality in male sexual activity. It appears clearly in these works that Lawrence feared destruction not solely by possessive women, but chiefly by hostile men. His lofty quest for a freer world where men can share eternal, unisexual love, ends in America; for he came to recognize that his idealization of manly love was a symptom of his lack of masculine identification. The way in which Lawrence learned to make his belated, impaired masculine identification is recorded in the tragic tones and obsessive imagery of everything he wrote—largely in response to the symbolic American continent—from 1924 until his relocation in Europe. One cannot miss the suggestions of personal grief over the meaning of his own work as it reflects the forced readjustment in his soul. Lawrence himself, at the end of the summer at Kiowa, thought of the three tales he had just written as a unified but sadly disturbing group. He wrote to his agent that the stories "will easily make a book of three novelettes. But not gay, alas." (*CL* 813) And telling a friend about them, he wrote: "They all are sad. After all, they're true to what is." (*CL* 814)

Lawrence's first story during this period is "St. Mawr," the tale which has attracted such disproportionate attention from warring critics.[3] In style it is close to Lawrence's immediately preceding work, and some disagreements over the tale's meaning and worth can be settled by noting that "St. Mawr" issues directly from Lawrence's self-dramatizing mode in the novels and travel writings of the 1919–24 period. The tale's conversational syntax and colloquial diction keep us mindful of a narrator's viewpoint. The author's own racy, theatrical tone —which F. R. Leavis has fully described—creates the personal consciousness that interprets all incidents, and the narrative voice presents characters and events with deliberate disregard for objectivity or verisimilitude. Instead, we are offered the entertainments of irony and fancifulness. Even the opening paragraphs set rigid limits to our interest in mimetic details and, instead, they direct our view to puzzling influences which beset Lou's and Rico's curiously flawed lives. Each person is characterized by the mystifying, half-comical failure that mars his every effort and desire. We accept the suggestion—enforced by the diction of suspense and super-naturalism that Lawrence spreads across the first page—that they suffer from an enchantment. Lawrence makes a gesture at a naturalistic explanation for their failings in marriage—theirs is "a nervous attachment, rather than a sexual love"—but their plight, however ordinary in real life, has an atmo-sphere of extraordinary significance which fully holds our attention. At no time is the reader concerned with what will become of the Carringtons' marriage; we assume that it will dissolve as soon as Lou can win release from the awful spell that makes her life so unreal to her, and we attend primarily to Lou's fantastic deliverance from "nonentity."

Developments in the story are guided by neither probabil-ity nor logical necessity. After a report of their long, fitful romance proving Lou's and Rico's unsuitability for each other, suddenly "there was a marriage," without further ex-planation from Lawrence. When Lou's sardonic mother ar-rives, we relish the trouble she will create by arbitrarily "being on the spot." Lou purchases St. Mawr, a killer stallion, for her husband to ride in the Park—an action which, as Graham Hough points out, is "crazily impossible." Most of the fiction, however, is a fabric of equally unlikely experi-ence. Actions of the greatest importance are undertaken al-most whimsically; circumstances and locations seem to mate-rialize when needed. With Lou and Rico closely following, Mrs. Witt transfers herself to a country house in a remote vil-lage, where she watches funerals from her drawing-room window and makes barbed observations about the cheapened "sting-a-ling-a-ling" of death. Yet, after pages of her Gor-gonish disaffection with all humanity, the wealthy and sophis-ticated Mrs. Witt falls in love with Lewis, the stallion's simpleton groom, and she proposes marriage, which he unhesitatingly refuses. Meanwhile, the stallion has maimed Rico; and in order to circumvent a threat to geld St. Mawr and destroy his dangerous spirit, Lou, her mother, the horse, and two grooms depart forever for America. In New Mexico, now minus St. Mawr and Lewis, who were dropped from the story at a ranch in Texas, the two women and their Indian retainer choose to live atop a mountain in a wilderness that is devastatingly uncongenial to human life.

Until their arrival at the ranch, St. Mawr is the dominant presence in the tale. The horse is nearly a character or a setting all by himself. A red-coated creature that appears illusionistically to be made of flames, St. Mawr's fiery appearance indicates a dangerous spirit, that is suggested also by his "wide terrible" black eyes. The human characters' lives are radically altered when the stallion enters their polite world. To Lou especially, St. Mawr gives the hint of another mode of existence, and she puzzles over his meaning:

> Why did he seem to her like some living background, into which she wanted to retreat? When he reared his head and neighed from his deep chest, like deep wind-bells resounding, she seemed to hear the echoes of another darker, more spacious, more dangerous, more splendid world than ours, that was beyond her. And there she wanted to go. (*T* 576)

To the casual reader St. Mawr is a turgidly exaggerated symbol of sexual potency, so that Lou's puzzlement over his meaning must seem dim-witted and unaccountable in such an otherwise bright-minded girl. Certainly, when she first sees St. Mawr at a stable near the Park, her approach has all the overtones of a sexual advance which suggest that Lou wants, not a horse, but a virile lover:

> "May I say *how do you do?*" she said to the horse,
> drawing a little nearer in her white, summery dress, and
> lifting her hand that glittered with emeralds and
> diamonds.
>
> He drifted away from her, as if some wind blew him.
> Then he ducked his head, and looked sideways at her,
> from his black, full eye.
>
> "I think I'm all right," she said, edging nearer, while
> he watched her.
>
> She laid her hand on his side, and gently stroked him.
> Then she stroked his shoulder, and then the hard, tense
> arch of his neck. And she was startled to feel the vivid
> heat of his life come through her, through the lacquer
> of red-gold gloss. So slippery with vivid, hot life! (*T*
> 564–65)

A simple interpretation of the symbolism is supported by
Lou's later conversation with her mother when both women
deplore men's sensual inadequacies, and Lou specifically contrasts St. Mawr's vitality to the "deadness" of human creatures, including herself. Yet, this apparent significance of the
horse is misleading, for St. Mawr is an aberrant stallion and
that is why Lou decides to buy him. The stabler warns her
that St. Mawr " 'is a special animal and needs a special sort of
touch' ":

> "Well—my lady—they raised him for stud purposes
> —but he didn't answer. There are horses like that: don't
> seem to fancy the mares, for some reason." (*T* 564)

The creature seems crazed with fear of any contact, repeatedly springing away from a touch "as if lightning exploded
in his four hoofs." Having killed two men before Lou buys
him, he soon maims two more as a consequence of their mis-
handling him. The stallion's conventional association with
sexual power is meaningful to Lou because as a symbol St.

Mawr also expresses her fear of catastrophe in sexual contact, revealing her sense of doom or fatality in the sexual impulse itself:

> The wild, brilliant, alert head of St. Mawr seemed to look at her out of another world. It was as if she had had a vision, as if the walls of her own world had suddenly melted away, leaving her in a great darkness, in the midst of which the large, brilliant eyes of that horse looked at her with demonish question, while his naked ears stood up like daggers from the naked lines of his inhuman head, and his great body glowed red with power.
>
> What was it? Almost like a god looking at her terribly out of the everlasting dark, she had felt the eyes of that horse; great, glowing, fearsome eyes, arched with a question, and containing a white blade of light like a threat. What was his non-human question, and his uncanny threat? She didn't know. He was some splendid demon, and she must worship him.
>
> She hid herself away from Rico. She could not bear the triviality and superficiality of her human relationships. Looming like some god out of the darkness was the head of that horse, with the wide, terrible, questioning eyes. And she felt that it forbade her to be her ordinary, commonplace self. It forbade her to be just Rico's wife, young Lady Carrington, and all that.
>
> It haunted her, the horse. It had looked at her as she had never been looked at before: terrible, gleaming, questioning eyes arching out of darkness, and backed by all the fire of that great ruddy body. What did it mean, and what ban did it put upon her? She felt it put a ban on her heart: wielded some uncanny authority over her, that she dared not, could not understand.
>
> No matter where she was, what she was doing, at the back of her consciousness loomed a great, over-aweing figure out of a dark background: St. Mawr, looking at

her without really seeing her, yet gleaming a question at her, from his wide terrible eyes, and gleaming a sort of menace, doom. Master of doom, he seemed to be! (*T* 565–66)

The foreboding meaning of St. Mawr that Lou "dared not, could not understand" is no simple sexual hunger that she has repressed. From the first of the tale, Lou is established as a sexually experienced and candid young woman. She has had several meaningless affairs with ineffectual lovers—Rico among them—whom she regards sardonically. That she has never accepted any but the lame and the halt, as it were, that she can view them all ironically and easily dismiss even her husband from her life without taking another lover, all point to her continuous withdrawal from sexual involvement. She does not hope for mature sexual fulfillment at any moment in the story, and she is happy to be a sexual being only after she has escaped from all human relations. Lou's responses to St. Mawr overtly express her unconscious sexual anxieties, and that is why the horse is like a revelation to her. She lives in the thrall of male aggression—her aversion to what she believes is real sex is the only explanation of the "spell" of "nonentity" over her life—and St. Mawr expresses symbolically the intense ambivalence of her fear and her anticipation of violation by a man. The horse is not a figure of simple sexual potency but of dangerously overwrought sexual inhibition.

In a central episode, Rico rides St. Mawr on a picnic into the Welsh countryside and the stallion is frightened by a dead snake; he rears up and Rico reins him back until the horse topples over, breaking the man's ribs and crushing his ankle. For Lou the horror lies not in the accident but in the spectacle of the beast that is symbolic of phallic thrashing and plunging:

Lou gave a loud, unnatural, horrible scream: she heard it herself, at the same time as she heard the crash of the falling horse. Then she saw a pale gold belly, and hoofs that worked and flashed in the air, and St. Mawr writhing, straining his head terrifically upwards, his great eyes starting from the naked lines of his nose. With a great neck arching cruelly from the ground, he was pulling frantically at the reins, which Rico still held tight. Yes, Rico, lying strangely sideways, his eyes also starting from his yellow-white face, among the heather, still clutched the reins.

Young Edwards was rushing forward, and circling round the writhing, immense horse, whose pale gold, inverted bulk seemed to fill the universe.

"Let him get up, Carrington! Let him get up!" he was yelling, darting warily near, to get the reins. Another spasmodic convulsion of the horse.

Horror! The young man reeled backwards with his face in his hands. He had got a kick in the face. Red blood running down his chin!

Lewis was there, on the ground, getting the reins out of Rico's hands. St. Mawr gave a great curve like a fish, spread his forefeet on the earth and reared his head, looking round in a ghastly fashion. His eyes were arched, his nostrils wide, his face ghastly in a sort of panic. He rested thus, seated with his forefeet planted and his face in panic, almost like some terrible lizard, for several moments. Then he heaved sickeningly to his feet, and stood convulsed, trembling. (*T* 610)

St. Mawr's frenzy rouses her terror of sexual violation, but the image also hints at another fear. The impotent St. Mawr's panicky effort is to regain his footing and his aloofness, to escape the clutch that holds him arched up and straining. One suspects that the emotion in the passage includes a male fear of coitus that could only be Lawrence's own. The possibility is increased by Lou's reflections after the event, for Lawrence's apocalyptic damnation of mankind stridently overrides Lou's thoughts. As she rides home after the accident, "she had a vision, a vision of evil," that fills three pages. Rico seems to her only the presumptuous fool who tried, like all the "glibly evil" people in the world, to put natural life under his own restraining power. But her nightmarish image of St. Mawr shows that natural life itself—insofar as the horse represents it—is infected by a basic, dangerous, "positive evil":

> It was something horrifying, something you could not escape from. It had come to her as in a vision, when she saw the pale gold belly of the stallion upturned, the hoofs working wildly, the wicked curved hams of the horse, and then the evil straining of that arched, fish-like neck, with the dilated eyes of the head. Thrown backwards, and working its hoofs in the air. Reversed, and purely evil.
>
> She saw the same in people. They were thrown backwards, and writhing with evil. And the rider, crushed, was still reining them down.
>
> What did it mean? Evil, evil, and a rapid return to the sordid chaos. Which was wrong, the horse or the rider? Or both? (*T* 612–13)

The upturned horse thrashing to unleash his powers evokes by itself the fearfulness of that image: Rico's absurd trammeling shows only how dangerous the horse is, not how evil Rico's restraints are. The emotion in the passage is governed by the lurid symbol of the plunging phallus. The constant suggestion of explosive force comes from the animal, and that potential, whether good or evil, is what interests Lou. Her attachment to the horse continues only while there is something "wrong" in him—that is, while his symbolic intimations re-

main threatening to her—and she can contemplate his meaning and prize him "like a god" only while his potency is held
in check. When St. Mawr eventually mates with the mares on
a ranch in Texas he becomes irrelevant to her, and to Lawrence as well, because his phallic symbolism is irrelevant without the terror over phallicism that has risen to consciousness
in Lou. The stallion's role ends and he abruptly disappears
from the story as Lou and her retinue move on to the Rocky
Mountains. There, her apotheosis occurs when she becomes
consciously like the turbulently inhibited stallion. At the
height of her self-awareness, as she drives toward the mountain ranch that will isolate her from humanity, she elects ab-
stinence as a holy service:

> "Because sex, mere sex, is repellent to me. I will never
> prostitute myself again. Unless something touches my
> very spirit, the very quick of me, I will stay alone, just
> alone. Alone, and give myself only to the unseen
> presences, serve only the other, unseen presences."
> She understood now the meaning of the Vestal Vir-
> gins, the Virgins of the holy fire in the old temples.
> They were symbolic of herself, of woman weary of the
> embrace of incompetent men, weary, weary, weary of
> all that, turning to unseen gods, the unseen spirits, the
> hidden fire, and devoting herself to that, and that alone.
> Receiving thence her pacification and her fulfillment.
> (*T* 671)

St. Mawr symbolized Lou's fearful awe of the holy fire of
sex. She succumbs to her awe and she glorifies deliberate virginity as her destiny. Lou's aversion to sexual contact is
shared and emphasized by man, woman, and beast throughout
the tale, afflicting even St. Mawr's groom, who reflects the
horse's misogyny. Lewis's mythy mind, which Lawrence in-
tends to be neither comic nor pathetic, reveals the fearfulness

underlying his own and St. Mawr's unnatural behavior. Welsh fairy tales remembered from childhood are as close as Lewis can come to stating his ascetic religious beliefs. He envies "the people in the moon" who can live forever because they avoid the fire that blinds and kindles humanity:

"Unless fire touches them, they never die. They see people live and they see people perish, and they say, people are only like twigs on a tree, you break them off the tree, and kindle fire with them. You made a fire of them, and they are gone, the fire is gone, everything is gone. But the people of the moon don't die, and fire is nothing to them. They look at it from the distance of the sky, and see it burning things up, people all appearing and disappearing like twigs that come in spring and you cut them in autumn and make a fire of them and they are gone. And they say: what do people matter? If you want to matter, you must become a moon-boy. Then all your life, fire can't blind you and people can't hurt you. Because at full moon you can join the moon people, and go through the air and pass any cool places, pass through rocks and through the trunks of trees, and when you come to people lying warm in bed, you punish them." (*T* 641–42)

Sexual experience and the threat of death are so closely linked in all the details of the tale that the narrative of Lou's actions becomes an allegory of flight from sexual involvement —that much is clear—but, ironically, it leads Lou toward a surer threat of death. Her mother, like a prophetic crone, foretells the significance of Lou's final retreat to the mountains. Mrs. Witt, rejected by Lewis and disappointed in all her hopes to be mastered by man or God, looks upon dying as a deliverance from this world's paltry unrealities. While watching a funeral, she tells Lou that she looks forward to a painful death, because only the extremity of pain in that experience can assure her that she ever really lived. Observing the burial of a country maid, she lectures her daughter: " 'Now listen to me, Louise: I want death to be real to me—not as it was to that young girl. I want it to hurt me, Louise. If it hurts me enough, I shall know I was alive.' " (*T* 626–27)

While Mrs. Witt does not receive her wish to be hurt by death, Lou's response to the landscape at the New Mexico ranch assures us that *she* cannot fail to suffer the sting it symbolically threatens. For the reader, the landscape lifts the veil from the dreadful reality of Lou's experience. When the story introduces the mountain setting as the threshold of her destiny, suddenly all elements of the narrator's irony vanish from the fiction. Lawrence's oblique, satiric tone changes into the author's direct, lyrical heightening of the emotional effects of the scene. The change in tone is made especially emphatic by an equally abrupt halt in the events, which up to this point had been gathering momentum toward a final, climactic incident. Important narrative incidents had been occurring at a faster pace, sharpening our suspense over the outcome of the story. But, displacing the anticipated narrative climax, a long passage that is descriptive and analytical rather than narrative receives the full weight of emphasis. The climax of Lou's adventure is simply her entry to this setting, where she takes her place in a recapitulated line of pioneers and settlers who were defeated in the wilderness by its savage, teeming energy.

More validly than the symbolic horse, the mountains offer Lou an escape from the evil, enchanted, fraudulent world that represents usual life in the tale. The landscape supplants St. Mawr in the iconography of the tale because Lawrence's insight precipitously carried him beyond the only, tentative resolution the horse could provide for the story: Lou, disdaining mankind, could spend her days on a ranch riding the stallion across desert plains in perpetual flight from the sensuality that St. Mawr threatens, her fear identified by his impotence. But the mountain landscape does not allow for similar equivocation about Lou's fate: disintegration impinges on her, and she worships it with willed abandon. " 'I am here, right deep in America, where there's a wild spirit wants me, a wild spirit more than men. And it doesn't want to save me either. It needs me. It craves for me. And to it, my sex is deep and sacred, deeper than I am, with a deep nature aware deep down of my sex. It saves me from cheapness.' " (*T* 688)

The setting (*T* 673–84) pictures the reductive power of inchoate nature, "the seething cauldron of lower life." The spirit of the place that Lou embraces is "the vast and unrelenting will of the swarming lower life, working forever against man's attempt at a higher life, a further created being." She chooses to live where an earlier woman settler had watched "the gods of those inner mountains" relentlessly tear away all her little improvements, and even her beliefs. The lightning, that is reminiscent of St. Mawr's explosive hoofs, left its "perfect scar, white and long as lightning itself" down the length of the majestic pine tree by her cabin. The uncontrollable forces of nature destroy "the illusion she cherished, of love, universal love. There was no love on this ranch. There was life, intense, bristling life, full of energy, but also, with an undertone of savage sordidness." The continued renewal of man's effort against the chaos of nature in the mountains fulfills human individuality—"man is only himself when he is fighting on and on, to overcome the sordidness"—but this statement of a redemptive philosophy, which disguises the pessimism of Lawrence's outlook, is just not dramatically relevant to Lou. She has come to the ranch to deliver herself to its rudimentary nature, not to get things done there. She does nothing but worshipfully confront the sexual annihilation that is pictured in the loveless, savage energy of the landscape. She projects onto the destructive wilderness a "spirit" that seems erotic and desiring—and she awaits the doom that it threatens.

The astonishing thing about "St. Mawr" is that Lou's action is presented as a glorious fulfillment of her sensual being. But one must feel about this that Lawrence inaccurately interprets Lou's anxieties over any suggestion of sexual experience. The story is inadequate intellectually to its complex materials, because Lawrence does not rationally understand what his story reveals. Nevertheless, his false statements register, however ineptly, part of the meaning of the fiction. His affirmation of a redemptive outcome to Lou's action is not true for the heroine but it signifies an emotion appropriate to his sense of his own undertaking in exploring his feelings. Lou's paean to "wild America" expresses the author's wish to glorify the male sexuality which the horse and landscape symbolize. Because Lawrence, like Lou, regards phallic potency with terror throughout the tale as a whole, his celebration of her doom shows that he expects the sacrifice to be redemptive for himself. At the bitter cost of sending his female persona to destruction, Lawrence tries to accept his notion of maleness.

The next tale written after "St. Mawr" shows the same narrative pattern of an elaborately dramatized subordination of woman to a glorified male potency that the author deeply fears. The second tale clarifies this ritual action as an allegory of Lawrence's difficulty of masculine identification. Until the female principle—and the chief character is hardly more than that vague abstraction—submits to sexually brutal force that seems to emanate from a divine source, the woman lives in

spellbound detachment from reality. When she does worshipfully submit, she is destroyed by the triumphant male power.

The masterful opening of "The Woman Who Rode
Away" gives us a view of the unnamed Woman's husband,
and it indicates that a failure has already occurred in their
marriage. "She had thought that this marriage, of all mar-
riages, would be an adventure. Not that the man himself was
exactly magical to her." Assuredly, she had reasons to con-
struct illusions of an unusual life. Lederman (only *he* is
named) appears unnervingly magical to us. Physically de-
formed, crazily energetic, "a little, wiry, twisted fellow,
twenty years older than herself," ignominiously born in a foreign land, he came to America where he somehow triumphed
over defeats and made a fortune in silver mines of the Sierra
Madre. His history is not evidence of his bourgeois common-
ness, though the facts might well be; his wizardry makes him
strange: "One of those human oddments there is no account-
ing for." (*T* 756–57)

After years of bachelorhood—"he had been thrown out
on the world, a little bachelor, at the age of ten"—he married
her, "the rather dazzling Californian girl from Berkeley"; and
"he admired his wife to extinction." He took her to his silver
mines in Chihuahua, and there the years went by meaning-
lessly for her. "Her conscious development had stopped mys-
teriously with her marriage, completely arrested. Her husband had never become real to her, neither mentally nor
physically." The weird dynamo of a husband jealously guards
her in the seclusion of their adobe outpost, where like a little
alchemist he continues to make money out of raising pigs
when the silver market drops. Occasionally, the glances of vis-
iting engineers suggest a desire to loot him of his dazed trea-
sure. But inexplicably he holds her in some "invincible slav-

ery"; against all her disaffection with her lot, "he kept his spell over her."

What finally leads her away is a new anticipation of a bizarre adventure. Hearing about savage Indians living in the recesses of the highest mountains, she rides off to seek the sacred, dangerous tribe of the Chilchuis, descendants of the Aztec kings. Her action is a repetition of whatever irrational motive led her into marriage with the gnome-like Lederman: "She was overcome by a foolish romanticism more unreal than a girl's. She felt it was her destiny to wander into the secret haunts of these timeless, mysterious, marvellous Indians of the mountains." (*T* 759) She does not go away to liberate herself from Lederman's spell, but, instead, to seek again among more threatening figures the same awesome experience that the wizard could not satisfactorily conjure. Willingly she is intercepted by the wild Indians, who lead her in a terrifying mountain climb through gloomy forests up onto the very ridge of the earth, where she gasps in the thin, icy air. For part of the journey she must scrabble across the rocks, demeaned by her fear and by the sure-footed natives. She is puzzled by her own intention to continue: "Yet what she wondered, all the time, was why she persisted in clinging and crawling along these mile-long sheets of rock. Why she did not hurl herself down, and have done! The world was below her." (*T* 767)

The narrative of repetitious events shows the woman encroaching upon dangers that are potential, imminent, arrested in threats or in omens of her destruction. From the dead dog lying in the road near her husband's mine to the Chilchui village that is forebodingly emptied and which "glittered white," her journey leads her continuously through images of doom. During her imprisonment the Indians drug her into deeper forgetfulness and elaborately prepare her for sacrifice on the day of the winter solstice in a cave that is sacred to the sun and moon. The final scene's glistening tooth of ice, stained red in the light of the December sun, the flint knives of the priests held above her outstretched naked body, all the lurid eroticism of the sacrifice makes it clear that the imminent death-stroke is the equivalent of coitus. The fiction draws this precise implication that the Woman compulsively seeks what is death to have.

But none of the story's portended violence *occurs*, and the fiction does not allow either the Woman's death or any modification of what impels her. Even the sacrificial thrust is arrested, in a conditional verb, as the tribe's dying chief waits for the descending sun: "Then the old man would strike, and strike home, accomplish the sacrifice and achieve the power." (*T* 788) The allegory is evidently about a state of ambivalence so intense that neither the desire for a demonic sexual experience nor the anxiety over its destructiveness can be dramatized by conclusive actions.

Lawrence, however, overlaid this intricate art-expression with a moral as deceptive as any pious cant he excoriated in Hawthorne. He offers the Indians' mythology as a figurative explanation of the tale's meaning. The supremacy of the Chilchui gods must be restored by liberating them from captivity by the white race, and the sacrifice of a white woman is necessary for this resuscitation of Indian manhood. The author interprets the ritual as a promise of essential, natural Being triumphing over the will and mentality of modern consciousness: "Her kind of womanhood, intensely personal and individual, was to be obliterated again, and the great primeval symbols were to tower once more over the fallen individual independence of woman. The sharpness and the quivering nervous consciousness of the highly-bred white woman was to be destroyed again, womanhood was to be cast once more into the great stream of impersonal sex and impersonal passion." (*T* 777) Critics and readers have noted that this argument is not supported by the story's facts.⁴ Lawrence's female characters who are strongly individual—Gertrude Morel, Miriam Leivers, Hermione Roddice, or Gudrun Brangwen—could be seen to typify "the sharpness and the quivering nervous consciousness of the highly-bred white woman," but the Woman in this story represents nothing of the sort. She is the most rudimentary human figure, barely capable of individual consciousness. She is of no personal interest to us, and her chief particularity is that her identity is blanked out like her name. Only the author could recognize in the Woman somebody who was "intensely personal and individual." She is his own persona, his maternal image of the unfulfilled feminine quality of his soul. She has been "absent" from her life even before her adventure begins, and on the first night of her journey into the mountains she recognizes that now she is "a woman who had died and passed beyond." She observes that she is undergoing a momentous change. Repeatedly during her captivity, the Woman falls into "a trance of her senses" after doses of Indian drugs that are literally psychedelic. By the time of the solstice, her "passional cosmic consciousness," as Lawrence calls it, "became the only state of consciousness she really recognized: this exquisite sense of bleeding out into the higher beauty and harmony of things." (*T* 779–80) When all her human particularity is completely dissolved the Woman is delivered toward a death that is symbolic of sexual violation.

The atmosphere of fascinated horror in the tale's emblematic conclusion cannot be associated with the Woman's own complexities or hesitations, because she has none. The ambiguity of tone indicates the author's own feelings of anticipation and revulsion over the meaning of the symbolic act. Lawrence seems compelled to go through with what appears dreadful to him—that is, he idealizes the very notion of manhood that makes masculinity frightening to him. Not only is part of his own soul to be destroyed, but he must learn to exercise the wild and savage power that he associates with male sexuality. His circumstance as an initiate in a rite of passage is figured by the Indian youth, the old priest's grandson and heir, who repeatedly attends the Woman during her imprisonment and views her with both covert sympathy and malice. Like an Oedipally-distressed son, his attachment to the willing victim is expressed by his confused sexual role in her presence and by his repressed fury:

> The young Indian would sit and talk with her freely, as if with great candour. But with him, too, she felt that everything real was unsaid. Perhaps it was unspeakable. His big dark eyes would rest on her almost cherishingly, touched with ecstasy, and his beautiful, slow languorous voice would trail out its simple, ungrammatical Spanish. . . .
> It was curious, he would sit with her by the hour, without ever making her self-conscious, or sex-conscious. He seemed to have no sex, as he sat there so still and gentle and apparently submissive, with his head bent a little forward, and the river of glistening hair streaming maidenly over his shoulders.
> Yet when she looked again, she saw his shoulders broad and powerful, his eyebrows black and level, the short, curved, obstinate black lashes over his lowered eyes, the small, fur-like line of moustache above his blackish, heavy lips, and the strong chin, and she knew

that in some other mysterious way he was darkly and powerfully male. And he, feeling her watching him, would glance up at her swiftly with a dark, lurking look in his eyes, which immediately he veiled with that half-sad smile. (*T* 774–75)

The subtly suggestive, silent intimacy between the youth and the Woman is reminiscent of young Paul Morel's moments of domestic company with his mother. When the Woman asks why the Indians hate her, this minor figure of boyish, impotent love-and-resentment reflects some of Paul's tortured attachment to Mrs. Morel:

> He looked up suddenly with a light on his face, and a startling flame of a smile.
> "No, we don't hate," he said softly, looking with a curious glitter into her face.
> "You do," she said, forlorn and hopeless.
> After a moment's silence, he rose and went away. (*T* 779)

The full ambiguity of this symbolic tale shows the severity of Lawrence's psychological plight. His murderous resentment against a maternal figure—a feeling that is dramatized in his work as early as *The Trespasser*—rouses guilt that further inhibits his manhood, especially since his image of maleness is an impersonally remote and brutally hostile sexual force. In the work of this summer he brings into sharper definition both his guilty antagonism against woman and his fearful obsession with male destructiveness. By confronting the irreducible dilemma in his soul, he imperiled his very sanity. Chaos loomed inside him, and the supposition that an equivalent chaos lay at the heart of all Nature continued to gain prominence in his themes and imagery.

The third tale of this summer's group enforces its own psychoanalytic interpretation of the horrendous sexual confrontation in the concluding episode. We are made to see the catastrophe in "The Princess" as the enactment of the heroine's ambivalently incestuous desires. Dollie Urquhart was raised by her crazy father to be the Princess in his fantasy of royal fairy people who are doomed to extinction. The two of them, he teaches her, are "the last of the royal race of the old people." Predictably, the child grows to be a sexless woman, beautiful but elfin: "not quite human." When she is thirty-eight, Colin Urquhart dies and the Princess is, in effect, widowed; and with some petulance she begins to think of having to make an actual marriage. At a dude ranch in New Mexico she is attracted by a young Mexican guide who is also the last of a noble line—his family once owned the vast tract on which he now works as a lackey for the American owners. In the dark glitter of Romero's eyes she rediscovers her father's aura of romantic doom, which renews her desire for an intimacy that is possible only at the verge of death:

> He gave her the feeling that death was not far from him. Perhaps he too was half in love with death. However that may be, the sense she had that death was not far from him made him "possible" to her. (*T* 700)

She induces him to guide her from the valley up to his mountain cabin "to see the wild-life," and there she invites their sexual intercourse, submitting to it with regret and detachment: "However, she had willed it to happen, and it had happened." Afterwards, her piercing disdain and revulsion drive Romero into a frenzy of brutality. After days of her powerless, horrified subjection to his bitter passion, her absolute resistance breaks even his will to conquer her. Then, they have accomplished their mutual destruction:

They were two people who had died. He did not
touch her any more. In the night she lay and shivered
like a dying dog. . . .
He went about in silence, with a dead-looking face. It
was now so dreary and so like death she wished he
would do anything rather than continue in this negation.
If now he asked her to go down with him to the world
and marry him, she would do it. What did it matter?
Nothing mattered any more.
But he would not ask her. His desire was dead and
heavy like ice within him. (*T* 722–23)

On the fourth day she is rescued by Forest Rangers who have
to shoot and kill Romero. The experience leaves the Princess
"slightly crazy," as she had always seemed to be. Later, having blocked out the memory of what actually happened to
her, "she married an elderly man, and seemed pleased."

The fey Princess and the sullen Mexican dramatize an apparently special case of distorted sensuality. Their characters
are shown to be formed by particular external circumstances.
Dollie's arrested sexual development is blamed on her father,
and Romero's debased manhood is the casualty of an economic conflict between populations. The assumed data give
Lawrence a rationale of abnormal psychology to diagnose
their responses and explain their actions. They are represented
as objects of clinical interest to him, and consequently the tale
seems lurid when the viewpoint dwells too long on any moment or detail of their personal drama. The story of "The
Princess" is more properly viewed from considerable aesthetic
distance, for it is like the romance of Gerald Crich and
Gudrun Brangwen re-enacted in Southwestern dress by a pair
of mental patients.

Detached from both principals in the tale, whom he pre-
judges as irrecoverably doomed souls, Lawrence draws close

to the setting, and he invests it with the tense complexities of feeling that indirectly pertain to the human characters. For thirteen pages of uninterrupted natural description—in a thirty-six-page story—the two figures on horseback ascend the Rockies. This extended presentation of the awesome landscape establishes the emotional context of their journey, for we associate its atmosphere of terror and curiosity with Dollie's sexual motive for the excursion. To some extent, the Princess identifies with the natural scene and she directs our interpretation of it as an image of her unconscious character: "And again the chill entered the Princess's heart as she realized what a tangle of decay and despair lay in the virgin forests." (*T* 704) In dizzying glimpses through the funnel-like canyons Dollie sees the floor of the desert slipping away to a tilted horizon. Amidst the mountain contours she seems to be encroaching upon a precipitous and irreducible conflict of natural forces. Ahead of her the summits are "grey," "dead," "corpse-like," and the "palely cold" wind blows "like some vast machine." The farther removed from the level earth, the sharper is her sense of "the inner chaos of the Rockies." When they reach the very top of the ridge, she quails at the revelation:

> In front now was nothing but mountains, ponderous, massive, down-sitting mountains, in a huge and intricate knot, empty of life or soul. Under the bristling black feathers of spruce nearby lay patches of white snow. The lifeless valleys were concaves of rock and spruce, the rounded summits and the hogbacked summits of grey rock crowded one behind the other like some monstrous herd in arrest.
> It frightened the Princess, it was *so* inhuman. She had not thought it could be so inhuman, so, as it were, anti-life. And yet now one of her desires was fulfilled. She

had seen it, the massive, gruesome, repellent core of the
Rockies. She saw it there beneath her eyes, in its gigan-
tic, heavy gruesomeness.

And she wanted to go back. At this moment she
wanted to turn back. She had looked down into the
intestinal knot of these mountains. She was frightened.
She wanted to go back.

But Romero was riding on. . . . . (*T* 711)

In this passage, as in both preceding tales, the emotions
present in the descriptive writing and the emphasis directed to
the surrealistically distorted landscape recall Lawrence's absorption with the fateful Alpine setting in *Women in Love*. In
that work it is Gudrun, whose erotic nature is largely Birkin's
disguised homosexuality, who recognizes with wonder and
ecstasy that the mountains symbolize her desire and fate. The
symbolic meaning of the mountains in the American tales becomes more closely identified with the author's own view of
general nature, while the women, represented as possessed,
drugged, or insane, become increasingly devalued and utterly
objectified by the author. The atmosphere of horror and
compulsion that is created entirely by the fictional characters
in *Women in Love* issues in these tales from the authorial response to the landscape and to the sexual acts that occur in
each "gruesome" setting. The recurrent symbol of mountain
landscape conveys much the same meaning in his art, but over
the years the symbol pertains less to characters and their actions and more directly to Lawrence himself.

In view of the clearly personal symbolism of the landscape
in the American tales, it is easier to see, retrospectively, the
consistency in all of Lawrence's references to symbolic mountains. The image is always expressive of a homosexual obsession with the power of brutal male force. In Lawrence's early

works, the obsession is in his characters; in his later works, the obsession is within the author. In "The Prussian Officer," a tale published in 1914, the homosexually responsive orderly kills his vicious Prussian officer and then dies within sight of luminous mountains on the horizon that retain, after he loses consciousness, the illumination "which was lost in him." (*T* 27–28) In "The Captain's Doll," which was written in 1921, Captain Hepburn must climb with Hannele to a picnic on a glacier; and there he must triumph over the awesome mountain-ice and reject its beauty, before he can win Hannele's agreement to marriage. In Lawrence's Introduction to Magnus's *Memoirs* the critical action occurs on the mountain slope as Lawrence tears himself away from "the poignancy of the not-quite-dead past." Vaguely, he associates the monastery and the clearly homosexual Magnus with a strong regressive impulse in his own nature. The flight from a symbolic mountain occurs in *Sea and Sardinia* also, where Lawrence ascribes witchcraft to Mt. Etna and tries futilely to escape it. The mountain's magic impels him to seek the companionship of other men, but he returns to its precincts bereft of all hope for comrades. These instances, together with the major symbolic mountain in *Women in Love*, show that Lawrence consistently projected his sexual fears into the same awesome, natural image; and he approached understanding of his sexual feelings as he recognized the meanings of that recurrent symbol. When, after extraordinary psychological preparations, he brought himself to live for an extended period amid the Rocky Mountains, he entered upon the ground that his own art had fated for a crisis of self-discovery. The New Mexico landscape—tortured as it is by relentless forces—was the symbol of his illumination and despair; it revealed himself and it expressed his altered conception of all *nature*.

His identification with the symbolic place is the reason that the Pan myth reappeared in his writings about the Southwest during the early summer of 1924.[5] He tried unsuccessfully to let that myth explain why the landscape near his ranch was like a "living" being to him, and why he described it with such complex feeling in his tales. In "Pan in America" especially, Lawrence affirms that the scene at Kiowa has an active relation with human character. Particularly the blazed and lightning-scarred pine tree which stands "fierce and bristling" in front of his cabin influences him at a very deep level:

> I am conscious that it helps to change me, vitally. I am even conscious that shivers of energy cross my living plasm from the tree, and I become a degree more like unto the tree, more bristling and turpentiney, in Pan. And the tree gets a certain shade and alertness of my life, within itself. (P 25)

But the Pan myth is too shallow and literary to clarify Lawrence's intense absorption with the Kiowa location. During the time he was writing the three Southwestern tales, he was also describing Indian ritual dances in three essays which are the expository counterparts to the fiction.[6] He felt that the Indians' animistic world-view kept them close to the varied realities of their own natures. In the essay on "Indians and Entertainment" (*Mornings*, 99–122) he points to the European's and the Oriental's interest in the drama as an indication of their wish to survey life distantly, as from the balcony of a theater looking safely down upon "the realm of actuality." The Indian knows no such detachment from experience and he has, in our sense, no entertainment; in his games, as in his ritual dances, he is "completely embedded in the wonder of his own drama." For him there is never a God serenely looking on, for his worship is a struggle to master the powers of many gods who dwell near men in the physical universe.

In "The Dance of the Sprouting Corn" (*Mornings*, 125–38) Lawrence tries to convey the cosmic consciousness that he ascribes to the Indians. The beginning of the essay describes the pueblo's desert location impressionistically: "Pale, dry, baked earth, that blows into dust of fine sand. Low hills of baked pale earth, sinking heavily, and speckled with dark dots of cedar bushes." The first eleven sentences, comprising more than three paragraphs, contain not a single verb that makes an independent clause or that draws attention to a particular observer. He directs our eyes only toward the scene, and the effect of the painterly manner is to associate the location with timelessness and infinite space. The whole cosmos seems to center where the Indians in brilliant costumes dance under a wide hot sky arching above a brown land. Ritually chanting and dancing, they once again induce the earth and sky into that conjunction which is the crest, or season, of a new creation. In the essay's schematic view, man, who is limited and overmatched by the forces of nature, is nevertheless the sensitive organizer of its powers which he uses to sustain him as the highest development of life.

The essays show Lawrence turning away from his former assumption that physical energies are naturally benign and that they issue creatively only in spontaneous, instinctive actions. The supposition that unconscious nature is by itself malign appears most clearly in the third of the series, "The Hopi Snake Dance" (*Mornings*, 141–79). The essay recounts his excursion to the Hopi's distant pueblo and it explains the symbolism of their ritual. With great care to include the dates, distances, hours, and all the authenticating details of this particular event, he describes the Indians' ritual to placate the dangerous spirits that lie hidden in nature. To Lawrence the ceremony typifies "the religion of aboriginal America"; it is his interpretation of their intuitive, direct knowledge of the meaning of the land.[7]

Chiefly, Lawrence is interested in the Indians' concept of "the dark sun" at the center of the earth, which they regard as "the terrific, terrible, crude Source" of all things. Energies streaming from it create the cosmos, which is "a vast and violent matrix where souls form like diamonds in earth, under extreme pressure." No design directs this continuous upwelling, and only each creature's efforts to govern the forces of life lead them into creative rather than destructive issue. The Hopi, who soothes the rattlesnake before letting it go back into the earth, knows that "cruelty is coiled in the very beginnings of all things, and circle after circle creation emerges towards a flickering, revealed Godhead." Man is "the farthest adventurer" in the eternal struggle to order the elements of nature. By knowledge and courage he can resist the chaos that threatens always to defeat him and draw him unwarily to destruction. But he must expose himself to direct contact with nature's dangerous energies and let them enter his conscious life:

> Man, little man, with his consciousness and his will, must both submit to the great origin-powers of his life, and conquer them. Conquered by man who has overcome his fears, the snakes must go back into the earth with his messages of tenderness, of request, and of power. They go back as rays of love to the dark heart of the first of suns. But they go back also as arrows shot clean by man's sapience and courage, into the resistant, malevolent heart of the earth's oldest, stubborn core. In the core of the first of suns, whence man draws his vitality, lies poison as bitter as the rattlesnake's. This

poison man must overcome, he must be master of its issue. Because from the first of suns come travelling the rays that make men strong and glad and gods who can range between the known and the unknown. Rays that quiver out of the earth as serpents do, naked with vitality. But each ray charged with poison for the unwary, the irreverent, and the cowardly. Awareness, wariness, is the first virtue in primitive man's morality. And his awareness must travel back and forth, back and forth, from the darkest origins out to the brightest edifices of creation. (*Mornings,* 173–74)

The Indians' religion was meaningful to Lawrence because they posited an ambiguous malevolence in nature's creative force. In his view, their manhood depended on their courage and strength to embrace nature's deadly power and bring it to the service of their own life. Their beliefs echoed the insights of his summer's fiction, for he had penetrated to psychic levels where he saw at the center of his universe—not a rainbow, but "poison bitter as the rattlesnake's." He too had to embrace its potency, and to cease his equivocation between sexual roles. In New Mexico he stood ready to accept his horrendous notion of the phallic power of manhood.

Four years later, after he had resumed residence in Europe because of his health, Lawrence recollected the sense of exaltation and deliverance that he experienced at Kiowa. The place itself had been a vehicle of change in his psychology, and he continued to regard it as a sacred location, where some important truth had been revealed to him:

> I think New Mexico was the greatest experience from the outside world that I have ever had. It certainly changed me for ever. . . .
> But the moment I saw the brilliant, proud morning shine high up over the deserts of Santa Fe, something

stood still in my soul, and I started to attend. . . . In the magnificent fierce morning of New Mexico one sprang awake, a new part of the soul woke up suddenly, and the old world gave way to a new.

There are all kinds of beauty in the world, thank God, though ugliness is homogeneous. How lovely is Sicily, with Calabria across the sea like an opal, and Etna with her snow in a world above and beyond! How lovely is Tuscany, with little red tulips wild among the corn; or bluebells at dusk in England, or mimosa in clouds of pure yellow among the grey-green dun foliage of Australia, under a soft, blue, unbreathed sky! But for a *greatness* of beauty I have never experienced anything like New Mexico. All those mornings when I went with a hoe along the ditch to the Cañon, at the ranch, and stood, in the fierce, proud silence of the Rockies, on their foothills, to look far over the desert to the blue mountains away in Arizona, blue as chalcedony, with the sage-brush desert sweeping grey-blue in between, dotted with tiny cube-crystals of houses, the vast amphitheatre of lofty, indomitable desert, sweeping round to the ponderous Sangre de Cristo, mountains on the east, and coming up flush at the pine-dotted foothills of the Rockies! What splendour! Only the tawny eagle could really sail out into the splendour of it all. Leo Stein once wrote to me: It is the most aesthetically-satisfying landscape I know. To me it was much more than that. It had a splendid silent terror, and a vast far-and-wide magnificence which made it way beyond mere aesthetic appreciation. Never is the light more pure and overweening than there, arching with a royalty almost cruel over the hollow, uptilted world. For it is curious that the land which has produced modern political democracy at its highest pitch should give one the greatest sense of overweening, terrible proudness and mercilessness: but so beautiful, God! so beautiful! Those that have spent morning after morning alone there pitched among the pines above the great proud world of desert will know, almost unbearably how beautiful it is, how clear and unquestioned is the might of the day. Just day itself is tremendous there. It is so easy to understand that the Aztecs gave hearts of men to the sun. For the sun is not merely hot or scorching, not at all. It is of a brilliant and unchallengeable purity and haughty serenity which would make one sacrifice the heart to it. Ah, yes, in New Mexico the heart is sacrificed to the sun and the human being is left stark, heartless, but undauntedly religious. (*P* 142–43)

The lapse of four years between the actual moment and his interpretation of its significance obscures Lawrence's state of exhaustion at the end of the summer. His letters show that at the time he was feeling tired, and also that he was complaining of chronic soreness in his chest and throat. In the autumn, just as he was completing the series of related tales and essays, he received news of his father's death. Evidently he suffered no visible distress over the event, but he mentioned it in the most elegaic context in a single letter—most appropriately—to Murry, whose role in Lawrence's emotional life subsumed the double figure of a friend-lover and father-rival. In reference to the betrayal of their friendship during the preceding Christmas season, Lawrence wanly forgives and dismisses the old rancor between them:

We shall never "drop in on one another" again; the ways go wide apart. Sometimes I regret that you didn't take me at what I am, last Christmas: and come here and take a different footing. But apparently you did what was in you: and I what is in me, I do it. . . .
The country here is very lovely at the moment. Aspens high on the mountains like a fleece of gold. *Ubi est ille Jason?* The scrub oak is dark red, and the wild birds are coming down to the desert. It is time to go

south.—Did I tell you my father died on Sept. 10th, the
day before my birthday?—The autumn always gets me
badly, as it breaks into colours. I want to go south,
where there is no autumn, where the cold doesn't
crouch over one like a snow-leopard waiting to pounce.
(CL 811–12)

The pathos in this letter suggests his willingness to settle
accounts and admit regrets with both his dead father and his
former friend. Wearied by sickness and intense work, Lawrence was also burdened by his more somber recognition of
himself and by his more conscious dread of male savagery. In
early October he made his third trip down to Mexico to complete a novel he had begun there more than a year earlier. In
that book, he would attempt a reconciliation of the conflicting attitudes that now openly contested in his soul.

7

"This high plateau
of death"

The psychologically decisive effort of writing *The Plumed
Serpent* made Lawrence regard the book, for a short time, as
"my most important novel, so far"—the one lying "nearer my
heart than any other work of mine." (CL 844-45) To many
readers for whom it is a ponderous and pretentious book,
Lawrence's special fondness for this novel seems weirdly mis-
placed. The fiction is a fantasy of the sort that Lawrence
could make profoundly beautiful in a short tale, but in this
long novel the laboriously sustained and minutely detailed implausibilities grow offensive. His overestimation of the work,
however, accurately reflects his feeling that the particular creative process from which it issued was a most important experience for him.

Like the women of the three preceding tales, Kate Leslie,
the heroine, delivers herself to violent forces connected with
the land—in this instance, to "the horror and climax of death-
rattles, which is Mexico." Years before, she divorced her first
husband to marry a renowned Irish revolutionary leader.
Now she feels that everything in her past was finished for her
when Leslie was killed in his fight "to *change* the world, to

make it freer, more alive." She has come to Mexico to escape from any further intimate connection with people or worldly activity. Wondering why she has chosen "this high plateau of death," she soon becomes oddly fascinated by the purposiveness of two revolutionaries, whom she blindly never associates with her dead husband. Kate joins with Don Ramon and Don Cipriano who revive the Aztec cult of Quetzalcoatl to supplant Christianity in Mexico. This nationalist folk-movement renews a "virginal" self in her; she dances with peasants, sings hymns of Quetzalcoatl which Ramon composes, and allows herself to be married to Cipriano, who requires that she remain passive during sexual intercourse. She agrees to become a goddess of earth and death in a new pantheon that includes Cipriano and Ramon, and she learns to accept even human sacrifice proudly without a shudder of revulsion.

The narrative is made up of many startling incidents of sacrifices, assaults, skirmishes, insurrections, betrayals, physical violations, and atrocious murders; but they are mostly emptied of any real frightfulness by the excess of violence. All the potential horror of the action is spent extravagantly in a swirl of foreground activity, leaving no sense of deep undercurrents of destructive motivations. The violence, as superficial as a comic-strip's, is overshadowed by the thematic patterning of the tumultuous narrative. The intention of the cult is to make motives into rituals, to dramatize essential human nature to the last varied detail. Ramon's hymns and sermons, which overweigh the novel with monotonous digressions from the story and characters, emphasize the reconciliation of all opposites in the principle of the living Quetzalcoatl, "the Lord of the Two Ways." As the chief god of the new worship, Quetzalcoatl symbolizes the union of male and female qualities singly represented by Cipriano, who is the living fire-god Huitzilopochtli, and Kate, the eternal Woman Malintzi. Substantiating the doctrine of the trinity, all nature offers symbolic examples of similar reconciliation of conflicting qualities in balanced co-operation. The sacred images in the new religion are rain falling on the earth, pre-dawn and twilight appearing between the night and day, Morning Star and Evening Star, fire in the darkness, the circle of the Lake of Sayula in the dry expanse of Mexico, and the union of co-ition.[1]

The main action of the fiction is the effort to elevate degraded human existence to a level where humanity is godlike. The new religion makes gods out of the principal characters and its designed effect on all believers is to rouse a conviction of their essential divinity. Lawrence uses realistic details of Mexican culture to represent the psychic degradation in which contemporary man lives, and the novel begins with two realistic chapters that establish his morbid repugnance for the world around him. The opening bullfight episode stresses the oppression of soul in a loutish mobocracy, and the climactic image for Lawrence's view of Mexican life is the maddened bull goring the anus of a picador's disabled horse while its bowels spill out. From such horror of brutal degeneracy, the novel eventually turns to describe a new religion of human redemption and transcendence.

Don Ramon, the savior-designate, is not disturbed by the circumstances of impoverished and exploited life within his society, and he is not impelled to change Mexico on the surface. He refuses an opportunity to become next in line for the national presidency, and his idea of social reform is to gather peasants together in farm-and-crafts communes where they make Quetzalcoatl costumes and learn the new hymns. His purpose is solely to revive the Aztec cult for the redemption of the Indian soul in Mexico. The one activity in life that he wants to change is sexual relations. He believes that the present practice of "letting oneself go" in sex involves a man ravishing a woman, or a woman ravishing a man: "There is such a thing as sin, and that's the centre of it. Men and women keep on ravishing one another. . . . Letting oneself go, is either ravishing or being ravished." (XVIII) From this center, sin spreads into all human relations, for they consist chiefly of people ravishing others and offering themselves for ravishment. His view of civilization is not far from the novel's emblematic opening picture of the horse and bull.

The religion he institutes centers in a ritual of sex and a sacrament of marriage that demand woman's "submission absolute, like the earth under the sky." Only her "supreme passivity" preserves gentleness in man and woman alike. Presumably, as individuals reject the disintegrative frenzy of sexual release, they organize the coherence of their inner natures. In a strange reversal of his earlier prescriptive views about sex, Lawrence implies that people can become serene and godlike as they learn to forgo orgasm and transcend the frictional passion of their ordinary intercourse.

The clay feet of the gods are never so embarrassing, however, as in the events on "Huitzilopochtli's Night," when Kate accepts her new role as Eternal Woman. The ceremony of Cipriano's apotheosis as the vengeful fire-god is the point late in the novel where the literal story line must be absorbed by the Aztec myth. Quetzalcoatl can be revivified in the fiction only as his legend comes to structure the characters' ensuing experience, but the myth never convincingly justifies the events that occur. The Catholic peasants who have attacked Ramon's hacienda and tried to kill him must be executed—not

by law, but by the will of the gods. Cipriano in body paint
and feathers stabs or strangles the victims, according to the
courage they displayed in the attack. The bodies are then laid
before the altar and Ramon as Quetzalcoatl accepts the offer-
ings. The whole of this elaborate and critically important
ritual does not succeed in sweeping Kate's imagination to a
new level of symbolic perception—and certainly not the
reader's either. Kate's immediate response is to find the ceremony brutal and loathsome, and the reader never forgets that
it is preposterous. Kate recognizes that in spite of all the costumes and liturgies Ramon and Cipriano "seemed nothing but
men." Her reaction indicates the failure of the symbolic elements of the novel to assert their meaning for us: "As is so
often the case with any spell, it did not bind her completely.
She was spell-bound, but not utterly acquiescent. In one
corner of her soul was revulsion and a touch of shame."
(XXIV)

The difficult effort of persuading her that the cult is meaningful is left to Kate's own specious reasoning. After witness-
ing the sacrifice, Kate sits brooding at home and she thinks to
herself that, after all, individualism is an illusion. She should
abandon herself in submission to Cipriano and fulfill her
generic Womanhood. At that moment Cipriano enters her
house and coaxes her to come to the church where they have
intercourse before the altar where the sacrificed bodies had
lain. Kate, continuing to cogitate uninterruptedly during
intercourse, finally accepts the role that she denied in the preceding pages:

> And she pressed him to her breast, convulsively. His
> innermost flame was always virginal, it was always the
> first time. And it made her again always a virgin girl.
> She could feel their two flames flowing together,

How else, she said to herself, is one to begin again, save by refinding one's virginity? And when one finds one's virginity, one realises one is among the gods. He is of the gods, and so am I. Why should I judge him! So, when she thought of him and his soldiers, tales of swift cruelty she had heard of him: when she remembered his stabbing the three helpless peons, she thought: Why should I judge him? He is of the gods. And when he comes to me he lays his pure, quick flame to mine, and every time I am a young girl again, and every time he takes the flower of my virginity, and I his. It leaves me insouciant like a young girl. What do I care if he kills people? His flame is young and clean. He is Huitzilopochtli, and I am Malintzi. What do I care, what Cipriano Viedma does or doesn't do? Or even what Kate Leslie does or doesn't do! (XXIV)

The context of the passage and the demands of the myth make Kate's sexual intercourse the very moment of her apotheosis. But her surprising transformation into Malintzi is accomplished only by her own casuistry. Her incredible mental detachment from her sexual experience at that instant is so bizarre that Lawrence's obvious fudging leaves us unconvinced of her new role.

Just before he completed *The Plumed Serpent*—and one would like to think it shows a twinge of artistic misgivings— Lawrence dashed off four travel essays about his daily life in Oaxaca that reveal him feeling sheepish as an author, perhaps already embarrassed by what he was driven to write in his Mexican novel. Later published as the first four chapters of *Mornings in Mexico*, the Oaxaca sketches each dramatize a single day during the week before Christmas. The opening comedy of "Corasmin and the Parrots" presents Lawrence full of laughter, finding man's pretensions, including his own, amazingly ridiculous. Men, like dogs and parrots, find it impossibly difficult to drop the gestures of self-importance which only parody their obvious limits and uniqueness. In the three other essays of the series Lawrence's witty, tolerant report of Mexican life continues to give mankind the lie in the teeth: all egotistical stances are self-evidently absurd when the ignorance, the frailty, the self-pity of an actual man are concretely shown. There was that grace of irony in Lawrence that could anticipate his repudiation of the overblown fantasy he was writing even while his emotional self had to pursue it to the end.

The whole symbolic effort of the novel is unsuccessful in respect to its religious and sexual formulations; Lawrence was simply incapable of deifying terror and slavery in sex. But the primary assertion in the conclusion of the novel depends on neither of these hypostatizations. Kate's personal attachment to Ramon and Cipriano together, and their mutual dependence on her, affirms the familial relations of child and parents that the mythology implies. She appears in the last chapters not as Malintzi but as a middle-aged woman fearful of loneliness, appreciative of calm, occasional sex, and connected to Mexico by love for both her husband and Ramon—who is represented in the Quetzalcoatl myth as a young god born from the principle of their marriage. In the conclusion of the narrative, Kate is reinstated with a husband whom this time she does not abandon for another. In Ramon she is given a mature son similar to her former boy-husband Leslie; and Ramon, unlike the earlier revolutionary, does not supplant an older man as her lover and end up dead in his usurpation. Kate in her final role promises motherly love to Ramon and perfect obedience to Cipriano. One successful effect of the deflation of exaggerated violence throughout the novel is that Kate is relieved of the dangerously attractive powers and betraying compulsions that accompany the sexual nature of Helena, Gertrude Morel, Ursula and Gudrun Brangwen, Lou Carrington, the nameless Woman, and the Princess. But *The Plumed Serpent* shows that, given Lawrence's views of the savagery of phallicism and the rapaciousness of independent women, his only recourse was to devalue sexual activity entirely, in favor of quiescence. The one myth in *The Plumed Serpent* that is fully supported by the author's feelings is the characters' descent from sexual exaltations to an aging, familial order of life.

Evidently, the details of the fiction are the symbolic facts of a psychological adjustment that Lawrence made in his own life. His subsequent writings suggest that after this winter in Mexico he no longer experienced feelings of sexual desire for either women or men, but that his libido was latent and narcissistic. The representation of sexual experience in his late works is sentimental and regressive, such as a man might conjure out of wishful memory. His worsened physical condition also probably precluded further sexual activity. His health broke under the long and immensely strained effort of writing *The Plumed Serpent*. When he finished it, he fell critically ill —"the very day I went down, as if shot in the intestines," he said. (CL 833) Tuberculosis flared openly from the chronic condition which he had long lived with and euphemistically referred to as bronchial inflammation. Now near death, he was moved to Mexico City for medical care and in the spring of 1925 he returned as an invalid to Kiowa where he recuperated. But on the journey he dictated to Frieda a fragment of a novel called "The Flying Fish" which reveals a surprising surge of joy in Lawrence, in spite of his illness. In the tale he appears relieved of bitterness, liberated from dread, happily independent of the outer world, and pleased with his own soul. The work shows a current of pleasure flowing back into Lawrence, after he threw off his burden of sex and the irreconcilable conflicts that it symbolized for him. He had cut his psychic losses, and his soul rose buoyantly with a new self-love. He later said that he would never be able to finish the story, for it was written "so near the borderline of death" that he could not "carry it through, in the cold light of day." [2] This explanation rings hollow, especially since Lawrence's best works in the remaining five years of his life were written in contemplation of imminent death. A sense of relief and a spirit of celebration characterize the whole tone of the fragment; "The Flying Fish" remained uncompleted because it is the outpouring of lyricism during an unrepeatable moment of self-acceptance—achieved, perhaps tragically, at whatever cost.

The narrative recounts the departure from Mexico of a malaria-ridden Englishman, Gethin Day, who is called home by the death of his sister, who was twenty years older than he and named *Lydia*, like Lawrence's mother. The death of this woman represents Lawrence's sense of release from the dominance of "a woman at the back of me," who was his anima, or feminine identification. Closely identified with his mother, she was the image of his internal nemesis, and Lawrence had long tried to kill her off in various matricidal fantasies recorded from *Sons and Lovers* through the three Southwestern tales. The woman's age, her name, her maternal resentment of Gethin's wandering about the world, and her steady subversion of his self-esteem, all continue Lawrence's equation between an older, sexually taboo woman and his own troublesome sexual ambiguity. In the tale Lydia had always reproached Gethin for not yet assuming his inherited, manly place in their ancestral estate:

This had always been the burden of her song to him: *if you knew how to come into your own.* And it had always exasperated him with a sense of futility; though whether his own futility or Lydia's, he had never made out. (P 781)

At last returning to accept his destined role, Gethin recalls long passages of mystic writing which he learned by memory from an Elizabethan chronicle of his family, *The Book of Days.* In a highly figurative rhetoric, the old religious writing plays with meanings of the "Greater Day" and the "lesser day"—which are man's levels of experience in spiritual and circumstantial worlds. According to the meditative Elizabethan, whose views now coincide with Gethin's new illumination, man's frenzied activity in the bright lesser day is only an escape from his fear of death. But in the Greater Day, which is a dark world of mystery, man can submit himself to death and learn the peace of joyful eternity:

> Even as the flying fish, when he leaves the air and recovereth his element in the depth, plunges and invisibly rejoices. So will tall men rejoice, after their flight of fear, through the thin air, pursued by death. For it is on wings of fear, sped from the mouth of death, that the flying fish riseth twinkling in the air, and rustles in astonishment silvery through the thin small day. But he dives again into the great peace of the deeper day, and under the belly of death, and passes into his own.
>
> . . .
>
> There is no help, O man. Fear gives thee wings like a bird, death comes after thee open-mouthed, and thou soarest on the wind like a fly. But thy flight is not far, and thy flying is not long. Thou art a fish of the timeless Ocean, and must needs fall back. Take heed lest thou break thyself in the fall! For death is not in dying, but in the fear. Cease then the struggle of the flight, and fall

back into the deep element where death is and is not, and life is not a fleeing away. It is a beauteous thing to live and to be alive. Live then in the Greater Day, and let the waters carry thee, and the flood bear thee along, and live, only live, no more of this hurrying away. (*P* 785–86, 788)

Gethin remarks after rereading this passage that he too had been hurrying away: "He had hurried perhaps a little too far, just over the edge." But the image of the flying fish and its reassuring meaning in *The Book of Days* come to him in his own experience as he sails across the Gulf of Mexico. The flying fish burst from the sea around the ship where Gethin watches them, and he gazes down at the running tip of the bow to recognize the unbounded freshness of the ocean:

> And below, as yet untouched, a moment ahead, always a moment ahead, and perfectly untouched, was the lovely green depth of the water, depth, deep, shallow-pale emerald above an under sapphire-green, dark and pale, blue and shimmer-green, two waters, many waters, one water, perfect in unison, one moment ahead of the ship's bows, so serene, fathomless and pure and free of time. (*P* 792)

Within that lovely, elusive ocean of life, the most exciting symbolic spectacle for Gethin is the school of porpoises who express a joyfulness that he had never met before. Gethin is entranced by their playfulness among themselves as they swim in ever varying yet unbroken formations:

> mingling among themselves in some strange single laughter of multiple consciousness, giving off the joy of life, sheer joy of life, togetherness in pure complete motion, many lusty-bodied fish enjoying one laugh of life, sheer togetherness, perfect as passion. They gave off into the water their marvellous joy of life, such as the man had never met before. And it left him wonder-struck. (*P* 794–95)

The change in Lawrence's unconscious appears in his delight with the symbols of ocean, fish, and porpoise—which are transformations of his recent images of dread, such as his deadly mountains, his feathered snake, and fiery stallion. The flying fish which rise up in needless fright express Lawrence's mastery of the terror that he revealed in the related image of the phallic, upturned St. Mawr straining with explosive power. The laughing porpoises know a joyful, innocent community that the death-and-sex rituals of Quetzalcoatl could not create in the preceding novel. And the essential unconscious takes the form of an "untouched" ocean, an "exquisite frail green" of "watery loveliness": there is not another landscape of mountain chaos in all the rest of Lawrence's work. Clearly, he had deflated the horror that had possessed his soul.

As soon as he felt sufficiently recuperated, Lawrence left Kiowa ranch in September 1925 and returned to Europe. In America, while writing largely in response to the American continent which was for him as for Kate "this high plateau of death," he accomplished as much as he could to uncover and allay the anxieties arising from sexual ambivalence which had structured his vision of life since his earliest works. In the years after his American experience he wrote frequently about a simpler, conceptual world patterned by his wishes, as in *Lady Chatterley's Lover;* his art no longer focused on the soul's violent conflicts between aversion and desire. Idyll and romance come to replace the intense psychic dramas that were his major effort in prose.

8

"An exit from the fallen self"

Less than a year before he died Lawrence completed a long essay defending his moral intention in *Lady Chatterley's Lover*. The separately issued pamphlet, *A Propos of "Lady Chatterley's Lover,"* is his best-written explanation of his views on sex, marriage and society.[1] It is a chastened, skeptical analysis of man's prospects for achieving harmony in himself and in civilization; like Whitman's *Democratic Vistas*, Lawrence's essay marks his deference to the historical future for that perfection of experience that he once sought to attain with his own efforts.

Lawrence states that in *Lady Chatterley* he purposely represents sex as it *might be*, not as it is; because our conscious attitudes made up of shame, guilt, boredom, or fear have made sex activity perverse. Given the catastrophe of our present sexual experience (the novel begins: "Ours is essentially a tragic age"), Lawrence advises that "Now our business is to realize sex. To-day the full conscious realization of sex is even more important than the act itself." It would perhaps be wise for young men and women to abstain temporarily from all sexual activity in order to let their mental understanding catch up with their bodies' experience. *Lady Chatterley* is meant to awaken new thoughts about sex:

> And this is the real point of this book. I want men and women to be able to think sex, fully, completely, honestly and cleanly.
> Even if we can't act sexually to our complete satisfaction, let us at least think sexually, complete and clear.
> (*P2* 489–90)

More than Lawrence's earlier works, this novel makes us *think* about sex. The fiction emphasizes the lovers' exact gestures, words, and conscious attitudes, attracting a gossipy sort of attention to the objective details of their sexual response. In contrast to *The Rainbow* and *Women in Love*, *Lady Chatterley* is concerned chiefly with its characters' conscious, not their unconscious, sensuality.

Connie Chatterley, as her father and other older men approvingly notice, is basically "old-fashioned" and womanly—which means that she is capable of deep submission to sensual experience. But because as a girl she accepted the current ideas about sex, she has come to misery in her mature life. By marrying Clifford she sought to retain "a pure and noble freedom" in love, believing that the sex attachment did not substantially alter or bind one's soul. When Clifford returned from the war paralyzed and impotent, Connie was doomed to the consequence implicit in her misguided choice. Her years of unfulfillment in marriage seem a cruelly wasteful penalty for her youthful mistake. She is completely deprived of warmhearted intimacy, and she has no place with the cleverly talking, passionless men of her husband's society. Clifford's paralysis is symbolic of his incapacity for genuine sympathy with other beings. His condition represents, for Lawrence, the maiming of man's emotions by our anti-sexual culture:

"He is a pure product of our civilization," Lawrence comments in *A Propos.* (*P2* 513)

Oliver Mellors, whose love changes Connie's life, also suffers from a disastrous marriage. In his youth he knew women who gave him their spirit of love but they never really wanted the physical act of sex; Mellors reacted from them by marrying Bertha Coutts, whose aggressions during intercourse finally demonstrated her fierce sexual hatred. Embittered against women and against modern industrial civilization, which he recognizes is anti-sexual, Mellors withdrew from the world to a hermit's life as a gamekeeper on the Chatterley estate. But he too is basically capable of tenderness and sensual love, and apparently he could have loved a girl like Connie even before he met her.

Both protagonists enjoy a single-minded favoritism from Lawrence. He idealizes them by keeping them free from serious complexities or shortcomings of character that might defeat their chance for happiness together. Mellors' love-making brings Connie gently into full sensual responsiveness. She becomes pregnant, openly acknowledges her affair with Mellors, and at the end of the novel the lovers are anticipating divorces which will enable them to marry each other. The story centers on Connie's steady growth into a fulfilled woman; her uncomplicated soul flowers like the woods in springtime where she meets with Mellors:

> She was gone in her own soft rapture, like a forest soughing with the dim, glad moan of spring, moving into bud. She could feel in the same world with her the man, the nameless man, moving on beautiful feet, beautiful in the phallic mystery. And in herself, in all her veins, she felt him and his child. His child was in all her veins, like a twilight.

. . .

She was like a forest, like the dark interlacing of the oak-wood, humming inaudibly with myriad unfolding buds. Meanwhile the birds of desire were asleep in the vast interlaced intricacy of her body. (X)

For Connie and Mellors sexual relations are sweeter and simpler than for any earlier pair of Lawrence's protagonists. They are the first major characters who are absolutely free of self-revulsion or any fear of sex, and the novel focuses attention on their sensuality. Lawrence describes their sexual intercourse in more explicit detail than in earlier fiction as he tries to purify every word and act of any shameful associations. He introduces the diction of vulgarity to the lovers' dialogues, and even Mellors' occasional preference for the "Italian way" is alluded to in the novel as unambiguously wholesome sex. The descriptions of their intercourse are not dominated by images of aggression, resistance, violation, or loss of identity, nor do the lovers struggle to orgasms of awesome intensity. In their rosy love the possible mischances are few and unimportant. On one occasion of their intercourse Connie remains derisively conscious of their movements and posture, and she feels terrible afterwards; but the pathetic failure has no effect on the narrative or on the sensibility of the characters, for at the very next moment Lawrence allows the lovers to easily regain the ecstasy that almost monotonously defines their sexual relations.

To represent characters who have perfect inner freedom for direct sensual fulfillment, Lawrence created a conventionally artificial world where the lovers could act according to his ideal of love rather than according to his knowledge of experience. Connie and Mellors live in the formal scheme of a pastoral idyll. Their love is dramatized only in the woods on the Chatterley estate, where rain falls softly through the dark-

ness or the twilight and the fresh growth of spring scents the
air. They dance naked in the glades and spread forest flowers
on their bodies. They make love in a forest hut or amidst the
undergrowth, and Connie returns in secrecy to her conventional place in the outer world. Anyone but the lovers enters
the woods as an intruding alien. The arrival of a postman at
Mellors' cottage and the return of Mellors' wife introduce
complications which threaten to defame their love—but no
circumstance can threaten the love itself. In this Arden also,
there is "No enemy, But winter and rough weather."

The ugly industrial works of the Chatterley coal-mines line
the rim of the forest, and in the manor-house the sophisticated
conversation of Clifford's vitiated friends displays the cyni-
cism of modern society. Meanness and perversity thrive in the
encircling world. As Connie matures into a sensual woman,
forfeiting her place in conventional society, Clifford becomes
a progressive business leader. Inwardly, however, he disinte-
grates to a state of child-like dependency upon his house-
keeper, Mrs. Bolton. While she kisses him all over his helpless
body, he fondles and kisses her breasts; and their regressive
eroticism contrasts with the vigorous sexual activity of Connie and Mellors. The difference between the innocence of
love in the forest and the decadence of experience in the
world is established with diagrammatic neatness throughout
the novel. Lawrence's attack against modern culture is only
superficial in *Lady Chatterley*, because the details representing its evils are obviously selected for their contrast to the
idealized romance, and not particularly for their reference to
an actual world. Far more artful and persuasive condemna-
tions of industrialism appear elsewhere in Lawrence's works;
for instance, in the twelfth chapter of *The Rainbow* which
describes the colliery town of Wiggiston while narrating the
marriage of Ursula's uncle and her lesbian schoolmistress.

Lawrence wrote three versions of *Lady Chatterley* as he felt the need to minimize realistic complications in the story and to create the world of idyll in the final version.² In each text he reduced the lovers' connection with society and made civilization's flaws less relevant to the lovers' future. From the first version he rejected the gamekeeper's virulence toward other people, as well as his lower-class uncouthness and his social radicalism as a secretary of a Communist League. He rejected the distressing conclusion of the second version, in which Connie and her lover are beset by a coarse, prying gamekeeper as Connie weeps desperately over their unlikely prospects for future happiness. In the third version, Mellors takes a job on a farm and prepares to receive Connie and their child when they return from Italy. His letter to her expresses confidence in their love, along with a stoical foreboding of social violence ahead for the rest of the world as a result of the "mass-will of people, wanting money and hating life." But he assures her that the inevitable ruin of humanity can have no effect on their destiny: "All the bad times that ever have been, haven't been able to blow the crocus out: not even the love of women. So they won't be able to blow out my wanting you, nor the little glow there is between you and me." (XIX)

Lawrence sentimentally implies that Connie and Mellors will remain free from the weight of misery and doom upon other people's lives. Throughout the novel the grief of complex passions and the reality of social life are alluded to, but only as vicissitudes the lovers have transcended. In their static idyll, Connie is always suffused with "soft rapture," and she is always yielding sweetly to Mellors' unflagging superpotency. *Lady Chatterley* shows what it might be like to know unending, unmixed sexual delight, and Lawrence discriminates and protects that ideal from the amalgam of actuality. His lovers, unlike those on Keats's Grecian urn, are congratulated for their fully consummated love; but both pastorals picture an idea of sustained perfection that contrasts with their explicit allusions to troubled human experience.

But even as a pastoral romance, *Lady Chatterley* fails in its effort to idealize love. Connie and Mellors show less awareness of each other and less belief in external reality than Lawrence's troubled characters display in his earlier, realistic fiction. Even though Connie and Mellors do not destructively pursue the mere sensations of *passion*, they are mere sensationalists, in Lawrence's sense, because they seek only release from the tension of individual being. They reduce love to manipulations that serve each other's pleasure. Contradictorily, Lawrence blesses them and at the same time abandons the world to its madness, condemning humanity for exactly such narcissism as the lovers reveal. David Holbrook, who has written at length about the distortions of love in this novel, argues that "Lawrence failed in *Lady Chatterley* to approach adult relationship at all, and loses his way altogether. He depicts a picture of neurotic genitality, conditioned by infantile oral aggressiveness. . . . He tries to solve the problem of love in terms of erotic pleasure merely." Holbrook demonstrates that the erotic pleasure which Lawrence celebrates in this book denies the object-relationship of love—and, fundamentally, it denies the object-relationship that supports a sense of reality. As Holbrook sees it, the novel is a schizophrenic performance entirely.[3]

The indulgent fantasy that generates this piece of fiction is Lawrence's uncritical identification with Mellors, whose impaired maleness Lawrence accepts as full manly development. The central concern of the novel is with him: Lady Chatterley's lover. His manhood is emphasized by its contrast with

Clifford's impotence, and by the carefully discriminated parallel between his sexual pleasure with Connie and Clifford's child-like happiness with Mrs. Bolton. Oliver Mellors is a refurbished Walter Morel—the name is not greatly changed—who is given license for the selfishness and abuse of others that Lawrence formerly feared in the generic nature of men. Mellors has unchecked possession of Connie's body which he adroitly and hostilely uses. No reverence for individual being enters his passion.

The direction of the narrative indicates that the ultimate goal of Mellors' pleasure-seeking is retrogressive freedom from all demands of sexual activity. At the end of the novel when Connie is pregnant, the lovers are separated but they anticipate "being together next year." In Mellors' famous letter, however, he states that the affair has already perfected his "chastity." He has had the relief of being able "to fuck oneself into peace." And now done with the process, he has left his intentions marked on the woman who served him. The child in her womb signifies his unconscious wish to be as infantile as Clifford fondled by his nurse. The apparent difference between the two male characters disappears when they both find fulfillment in voluptuous passivity.

From the tales contemporary with *Lady Chatterley* to "The Man Who Died," which is his last completed work of fiction, Lawrence displays impatience with the complex details of objective reality. Solipsistic and weary, he is more inclined to assault our ideas than represent our lives. In allegories, parables, and minor satirical sketches, he seems content to ridicule social behavior and judgments. Much of his poetry of this period—in *Pansies*, *Nettles*, and *More Pansies*—is prosy verse that expresses a moment's irritation with the vulgarity or evil of our common experience. But he was more apt to dismiss common experience than to sustain even negative emotions about it, and consequently the poems and fiction are generally slight or inept.

So thoroughly did Lawrence renounce his former commitment to perfecting human relationships that he reinterpreted the resurrection of Christ as a parable of his own renunciation of all external entanglements. In "The Man Who Died" the risen Christ disavows his previous gospel of love and wants only to be left alone. The Man turns away from his astonished disciples and wanders off aimlessly through a calm and sunlit Mediterranean world, slowly acquiring the satisfactions of taking his "single way in life":

> So he went his way, and was alone. But the way of the world was past belief, as he saw the strange entanglement of passions and circumstance and compulsion everywhere, but always the dread insomnia of compulsion. It was fear, the ultimate fear of death, that made men mad. So always he must move on, for if he stayed, his neighbours wound the strangling of their fear and bullying round him. There was nothing he could touch, for all, in a mad assertion of the ego, wanted to put a compulsion upon a man, upon all men. For men and women alike were mad with the egoistic fear of their own nothingness. And he thought of his own mission, how he had tried to lay the compulsion of love on all men. And the old nausea came back on him. For there was no contact without a subtle attempt to inflict a compulsion. And already he had been compelled even into death. The nausea of the old wound broke out afresh, and he looked again on the world with repulsion, dreading its mean contacts. (T 1115–16)

He comes upon a priestess of Isis, the goddess who waits to resurrect the dismembered body of Osiris. The young woman's ministrations ease the pain from his old death-wounds, and he responds to "her tender desire for him, like sunshine, so soft and still." Slowly wakening to their pristine desire, they have sexual intercourse—after the surprised Man exclaims with ludicrously literal reference: "I am risen!" The priestess becomes pregnant, as is her destiny. The Man, however, not wishing to be ensnared in "the little life of jealousy and property," sails away again in his little boat. He has fulfilled and left his mortal self in the womb of the mild-mannered woman; and sitting alone in the sexually symbolic vessel, the god happily muses: "I have sowed the seed of my life and my resurrection." Identified with the Creator by his fatherhood, the serene figure on the open sea forever escapes the demands or anxieties of being any particular, adult, separate person.

The tale elevates Lawrence's evident regressive tendency and presents it as the Man's holy renunciation of circumstantial experience. He passes beyond all human relationships to a connection with the divine world as a whole. The Man's religious devotion to cosmic rather than human life is supported by the tale's language, which is unusually stately for Lawrence. The dialogues are stilted, as befits the archaic characters. The Mediterranean setting is established by generalized and conventional details of sea-space diffused with bright light. Lawrence emphasizes the light, the wind, the crest and tints of the wide water, all in painterly expanses: "The sea was dark, almost indigo, running away from the land, and crested with white. The hand of the wind brushed it strangely with shadow, as it brushed the olives of the slope with silver." (*T* 1116) His description has the atmospheric effect of reducing vision to the sparest, stylized details: the writing reveals little empirical interest in the complexity of a particularized locale.

In *Apocalypse,* an unfinished study that was composed concurrently with "The Man Who Died," Lawrence discusses the Book of Revelation to show that Christianity as a social force is "the religion of the self-glorification of the weak, the reign of the pseudo-humble." The will to wreak destruction on the mighty—the apocalyptic vision—arises from a debased individualism, and a horror of one's weakness and isolation in the universe. In his eloquent peroration that is often quoted misleadingly to sum up Lawrence's life-long outlook, his former feelings of outrage and urgency have vanished from his analysis of man's error and frailty. The tone expresses awe for "the vast marvel" of being alive; and complementing yet differing from that awe, there is also his stoical acceptance of the imperfection and tenuousness of our connection with outer reality:

> For man, the vast marvel is to be alive. For man, as for flower and beast and bird, the supreme triumph is to be most vividly, most perfectly alive. Whatever the unborn and the dead may know, they cannot know the beauty, the marvel of being alive in the flesh. The dead may look after the afterwards. But the magnificent here and now of life in the flesh is ours, and ours alone, and ours only for a time. We ought to dance with rapture that we should be alive and in the flesh, and part of the living, incarnate cosmos. I am part of the sun as my eye is part of me. That I am part of the earth my feet know perfectly, and my blood is part of the sea. My soul knows that I am part of the human race, my soul is an organic part of the great human soul, as my spirit is part of my nation. In my own very self, I am part of my family. There is nothing of me that is alone and absolute except my mind, and we shall find that the mind has no existence by itself, it is only the glitter of the sun on the surface of the waters.

So that my individualism is really an illusion. I am a
part of the great whole, and I can never escape. But I
can deny my connections, break them, and become a
fragment. Then I am wretched.

What we want is to destroy our false, inorganic connections, especially those related to money, and re-
establish the living organic connections, with the cosmos, the sun and earth, with mankind and nation and
family. Start with the sun, and the rest will slowly,
slowly happen.[4]

No longer believing in direct action to change our political
or sexual life, Lawrence reaffirmed his vision of a newer
world in a rhetoric marked by vague gestures of hope: what
we *want* is to *start*, and to *know* that *the rest* will *slowly happen*. He secures himself in the generality and abstraction of
his sentiment about "the great whole," because even in these
last months, Lawrence could not contemplate specific object-
relationships without reviving his sexually-based fear of domi-
nation by others.

The current of Lawrence's imagination turned entirely in-
ward, and his significant artistic achievements in his last years
arose from an almost saintly contemplation of his own dying.
A group of death-poems from his posthumously collected
Last Poems together with his piece of graveyard literature,
Etruscan Places, comprise the best of his late works. In these
pieces, in which Lawrence confronts the solitary experience
that alone is real to him any more, he regains his splendid sensitivity to intricate life.

In *Etruscan Places*[5] he recounts his tour of the Etrurian
cities of the dead, tombs where corpses were provided with all
the accoutrements necessary for a continuing life. He is particularly interested in the paintings on the tomb-walls and in
the pottery that had been removed to museums, which he also

visits. Intermittently through the account Lawrence points up the irony of their survival amidst the stirrings of Mussolini's fascism in contemporary Italy. Most of Etruscan culture is lost to us because the civilization was crushed by the Romans' early power-drive. The Etruscan language was once as familiar to Romans as French to modern Europeans, but now the inscriptions are a mystery to scholars. Etruscan art was once precious to wealthy Roman collectors, but in Lawrence's day it was undervalued even by the museums that preserved it. Yet, the Etruscan element of vitality lives on in the pulse of the Italian people, Lawrence says, far more vividly than the Roman principles of dominion and riches, despite the fascists' attempt to revive Latin-Roman ideals. "Destiny," he remarks, "is a queer thing." The theme of his book is that delicately sensitive life, even in plants, outlasts the ravages of brute force:

> It is all a question of sensitiveness. Brute force and overbearing may make a terrific effect. But in the end, that which lives lives by delicate sensitiveness. If it were a question of brute force, not a single human baby would survive for a fortnight. It is the grass of the field, most frail of all things, that supports all life all the time. (52–53)

The Etruscans, Lawrence demonstrates, had the sensitiveness that gives their art universal meaning, despite their neglect of formal aesthetic perfection. Their temples, he points out, were "small and dainty in proportion, and fresh, somehow charming instead of impressive. There seems to have been in the Etruscan instinct a real desire to preserve the natural humour of life." (48) Their vases, too, express a spontaneous cheer and liveliness that is missing from more carefully crafted works:

If one looks for the Greek form of elegance and convention, those elegant "still-unravished brides of quietness," one is disappointed. But get over the strange desire we have for elegant convention, and the vases and dishes of the Etruscans, especially many of the black bucchero ware, begin to open out like strange flowers, black flowers with all the softness and the rebellion of life against convention, or red-and-black flowers painted with amusing free, bold designs. It is there nearly always in Etruscan things, the naturalness verging on the commonplace, but usually missing it, and often achieving an originality so free and bold, and so fresh, that we, who love convention and things "reduced to a norm," call it a bastard art, and commonplace.

It is useless to look in Etruscan things for "uplift." If you want uplift, go to the Greek and the Gothic. If you want mass, go to the Roman. But if you love the odd spontaneous forms that are never to be standardized, go to the Etruscans. (58)

In the painted tombs of Tarquinia, Lawrence responds to a reflection of his own method and intention in art, as Christopher Hassall has pointed out.[6] The delicate flowing quality of Etruscan paintings symbolizes their awareness of spontaneous, natural being underlying the outward shapes of things:

The subtlety of Etruscan painting, as of Chinese and Hindu, lies in the wonderfully suggestive *edge* of the figures. It is not outlined. It is not what we call "drawing." It is the flowing contour where the body suddenly leaves off, upon the atmosphere. The Etruscan artist seems to have seen living things surging from their own centre to their own surface. And the curving and contour of the silhouette-edge suggests the whole movement of the modelling within. There is actually no modelling. The figures are painted in the flat. Yet they seem of a full, almost turgid muscularity. (112)

The evidence of the Etruscans' modest, calm joy in themselves must have been an especial relief to Lawrence after his exposure to the grotesque and monumental art of the Aztecs in Mexico. Turning from the Indian awe of death—that had heightened his own—Lawrence was soothed by the Etruscans' absorbed satisfaction in their bodily existence. Evidently they felt no horror or poignancy over their transience, for their art rejoices in the frailty and evanescence of all life-images. Ordinary life was robustly enhanced by its ephemeralness, and death was only a continuation of that quality of daily existence. Their knowledge of death's mode in life gave grace and vividness to their individual, sensual perceptions. For them, as Lawrence interprets their tombs, death was the quickness, the subtlety of the life-experience. As he climbs in and out of their burial caverns dug under the hillsides or covered with mounds of earth, hurrying across the daylight from one dark descent to another, he discovers only beauty and truth to life in the images of oblivion:

> The tombs seem so easy and friendly, cut out of rock underground. One does not feel oppressed, descending into them. It must be partly owing to the peculiar charm of natural proportion which is in all Etruscan things of the unspoilt, unromanized centuries. There is a simplicity, combined with a most peculiar, free-breasted naturalness and spontaneity, in the shapes and movements of the underworld walls and spaces, that at once reassures the spirit. The Greeks sought to make an impression, and Gothic still more seeks to impress the mind. The Etruscans, no. The things they did, in their easy centuries, are as natural and as easy as breathing. They leave the breast breathing freely and pleasantly, with a certain fullness of life. Even the tombs. And that is the true Etruscan quality: ease, naturalness, and an

abundance of life, no need to force the mind or the soul in any direction.

And death, to the Etruscan, was a pleasant continuance of life, with jewels and wine and flutes playing for the dance. It was neither an ecstasy of bliss, a heaven, nor a purgatory of torment. It was just a natural continuance of the fullness of life. Everything was in terms of life, of living.

Yet everything Etruscan, save the tombs, has been wiped out. It seems strange. One goes out again into the April sunshine, into the sunken road between the soft, grassy-mounded tombs, and as one passes one glances down the steps at the doorless doorways of tombs. It is so still and pleasant and cheerful. The place is so soothing. (26–27)

Etruscan Places gives Lawrence an occasion for explicitly rejecting the views that his persona, Rawdon Lilly, upheld in his other "Italian" book, *Aaron's Rod*. In Lilly's final dogmatic address to Aaron, he insists that man must " 'accept the power-motive, accept it in deep responsibility. . . . It is a great life motive. It was that great dark power-urge which kept Egypt so intensely living for so many centuries.' " But in *Etruscan Places,* with its running commentary on Mussolini's fascism, Lawrence ascribes the futile power-motive to a desperate fear of death, and he criticizes those art-forms like the Egyptian which by mass, convention, and perfected formalism shut out our awareness of death that should enrich our daily lives. He finds in the Etruscan preparations for a continuing existence the images, the mood and the strength to express his own passage. The new influence on his imagination can be discerned even in "Butterfly," though the poem makes no reference to Etruscans. Its relation to the travel book is entirely a matter of Lawrence's feeling for the butterfly's delicacy and evanescence as auguries of his mortality:

> Butterfly, the wind blows sea-ward, strong beyond the
>   garden wall!
> Butterfly, why do you settle on my shoe, and sip the dirt
>   on my shoe,
> Lifting your veined wings, lifting them? big white butterfly?
>
> Already it is October, and the wind blows strong to the sea
> from the hills where snow must have fallen, the wind is
>   polished with snow.
> Here in the garden, with red geraniums, it is warm, it is
>   warm
> but the wind blows strong to sea-ward, white butterfly,
>   content on my shoe!
>
> Will you go, will you go from my warm house?
> Will you climb on your big soft wings, black-dotted,
> as up an invisible rainbow, an arch
> till the wind slides you sheer from the arch-crest
> and in a strange level fluttering you go out to sea-ward,
>   white speck!
>
> Farewell, farewell, lost soul!
> you have melted in the crystalline distance,
> it is enough! I saw you vanish into air.

Lawrence does not develop the poetic image much beyond its traditional banal meaning, but in the context of his life the poem is interesting because of its relaxed tone and Lawrence's refusal to interpret the image with explicit statement, as in "Snake," or with symbolic drama, as in "Cherry Robbers," two superior earlier poems. It is possible that he was trying to achieve the archaic, "flat" suggestiveness that he admired in Etruscan painting.

The Etruscan experience unquestionably underlies his major death-poems written in southern France. His recent descents to the ancient tombs are treated with mythological imagery in "Bavarian Gentians," one of his most startling innovative successes. The effort of his style is to make speech so symbolic that his individual words directly express a state of consciousness, without first being metaphors or symbols that refer primarily to the external world. By intensive repetition of key words—*blue, dark* and *torch*—he breaks down and transcends the descriptive and referential limitations of language:

> Not every man has gentians in his house
> in soft September, at slow, sad Michaelmas.
>
> Bavarian gentians, big and dark, only dark
> darkening the day-time, torch-like with the smoking
>   blueness of Pluto's gloom,
> ribbed and torch-like, with their blaze of darkness
>   spread blue
> down flattening into points, flattened under the
>   sweep of white day
> torch-flower of the blue-smoking darkness, Pluto's
>   dark-blue daze,
> black lamps from the halls of Dis, burning dark blue
> giving off darkness, blue darkness, as Demeter's pale
>   lamps give off light,
> lead me then, lead the way.
>
> Reach me a gentian, give me a torch!
> let me guide myself with the blue, forked torch of
>   this flower
> down the darker and darker stairs, where blue is
>   darkened on blueness
> even where Persephone goes, just now, from the frosted
>   September
> to the sightless realm where darkness is awake upon
>   the dark
> and Persephone herself is but a voice

or a darkness invisible enfolded in the deeper dark
of the arms Plutonic, and pierced with the passion of
    dense gloom,
among the splendour of torches of darkness, shedding
    darkness on the lost bride and her groom.

The poem intentionally separates two planes of reality by
using two kinds of language in opposition. The casual self-
effacement of the opening lines ironically undervalues the
poet's objective situation, and the more weighty emotional
terms of the second line allow his mood to dominate the scene.
Objective circumstances appear reflected in simple, logical
statements in which they are only marginally, laterally developed. The room, the flowers, the time of year remain at the
edges of the poem's field of awareness, where they frame the
central, imagined world of oblivion. The actual situation is
mildly reasserted in "frosted September," in the imperatives,
and in the analytically decoded—*dis-charged*—metaphor:
"Reach me a gentian, give me a torch!/let me guide myself
with the blue, forked torch of this flower." The world from
which the poet is ready to depart is relegated to a subordinate
level of reality, to a periphery of less intense consciousness.

For the central experience in the poem Lawrence uses language that is laden with compound adjectives and adjective
clauses. The elaborate modifications tend to dissociate darkness as a substantial, complex quantity apart from the flower.
It is darkness which suggests fire, smoke, light of the underworld, and the myth of the soul's descent to oblivion and
sensual experience in the deepest cavern of the earth. The
qualifying constructions build on each other, as seemingly
autonomous words crowd together in incremental, proliferat-
ing contact. *Dark* leads to "dark darkening," to "blaze of

darkness," to "darker and darker" and other variations. Each sentence extends further and further away from the influence of the simple grammatical base that refers to the actual situation. The amount and density of modification breaks down the normal syntactical patterns that preserve the duality of objective circumstances and a perceiving intelligence. Modification in this poem replaces verbs, so that adjectives function as whole predicates and appear as acts of mind.

No other commonly known English poem achieves an equally direct, sustained expression of almost unalloyed subjectivism. In "Bavarian Gentians" the world of fantasy becomes the substantive reality, the Nature in which we live. Only the mythological metaphor connects Lawrence with a world of similar fantasies about death. It is clear from his last poems that his sense of utter enclosure in private sensations threatened to demoralize him, but the exploration of death was his last connection with reality and he strove to remain aware of the experience he endured. He was conscious of the deliberate moral exercise required—the need for prayer—to see that death still linked him to the principle of life. In minor, meditative poems—"The Hands of God," "Abysmal Immortality," "Only Man"—his prayer is the same in each: "Let me never know myself apart from the living God!" (*CP* 699) He prevented his deterioration into complete solipsism that would separate him from even the symbolic cosmos:

> For the knowledge of the self-apart-from-God
> is an abyss down which the soul can slip
> writhing and twisting in all the revolutions
> of the unfinished plunge
> of self-awareness, now apart from God, falling
> fathomless, fathomless, self-consciousness wriggling

> writhing deeper and deeper in all the minutiae of
>   self-knowledge, downwards, exhaustive,
> yet never, never coming to the bottom, for there is
>   no bottom. (CP 701)

He escaped none of the woe of dying, not even when he could look confidently at his death as part of the universal process of growth, decay, and new generation. Small poems, written in the prosaic, spontaneous manner of his *Pansies*, express a moment's fear or misery:

Difficult Death

> It is not easy to die, O it is not easy
> to die the death.

> For death comes when he will
> not when we will him.

> And we can be dying, dying, dying
> and longing utterly to die
> yet death will not come.

> So build your ship of death, and let the soul drift
> to dark oblivion.
> Maybe life is still our portion
> after the bitter passage of oblivion. (CP 720–21)

The tiny "ship of death" that the Etruscans placed in their tombs for the soul's journey to another life was an entrancing symbol to Lawrence. The image recurs in many of his last works, and it provides the controlling metaphor and the title of his finest death-poem. In "The Ship of Death" (CP 716–20) he encompasses all his conflicting feelings about death, and he connects his experience with his life-long, complex vision of man's place in the natural world. The poem crystallizes his sense of the delicate balance between man's freedom in conscious action and his dependence on biological and

psychic forces greater than his deliberate will. Though the
tone varies widely through the ten numbered sections of the
poem, Lawrence sustains a dominant attitude of reverence for
the impersonal energies and universal events of mortal life.
The elliptical compression of the opening lines avoids the suggestion of merely private response by omitting personal nomi-
natives and by making verbs predicate only impersonal actions.
The subject of death enters the poem as a heavy gravitation
drawing all of nature downward:

I
Now it is autumn and the falling fruit
and the long journey towards oblivion.

The apples falling like great drops of dew
to bruise themselves an exit from themselves.

And it is time to go, to bid farewell
to one's own self, and find an exit
from the fallen self.

II
Have you built your ship of death, O have you?
O build your ship of death, for you will need it.

The grim frost is at hand, when the apples will fall
thick, almost thundrous, on the hardened earth.

And death is on the air like a smell of ashes!
Ah! can't you smell it?

And in the bruised body, the frightened soul
finds itself shrinking, wincing from the cold
that blows upon it through the orifices.

The first two sections establish both the natural dignity and
the individual pathos of the death-experience, and the complexity of articulated feeling is an extraordinary technical

achievement. The lines seem short and supple, yet stately, because they are organized by soft stresses overlaying a rippling, varied syllable rhythm—that is a nearly regular ten-syllable measure. The diction is simple, and the rhetoric is sometimes disarmingly conversational—as in "Ah! can't you smell it?" Autumn's conventional association with death receives fresh meaning from the striking development of metaphor. Lawrence brings a very free play of images into conceptual richness and unity that transcend the logic of paraphrase: the falling of the fruit becomes the general emblem of the apples that fall like dew onto the frost-hard earth and cold wind, there to bruise an exit from the body for the frail soul's impending journey over the ocean to oblivion.

The soul is "frightened," "shrinking," "wincing," and pathetically reluctant to face the inevitable departure; and as a possible evasion of the difficulty of dying, Lawrence contemplates suicide in sections III and IV. The question and answer rhetoric together with the insistent punning on Hamlet's term "quietus" and the "quiet" of nobly dying reduce the idea of suicide to a febrile, egotistical denial of the last, greatest event of life.

Aware of its life oozing from the cruel bruise and conscious of the dark flood of death that "is washing through the breaches of our wounds," the soul prepares a diminutive ark, with little oars and little cakes, even "little cooking pans/and change of clothes." The Lilliputian dimensions in this solemn, partly Biblical context can be a distressing preciosity to readers who want to feel glorified by man's tragic confrontation with an invincible enemy. But for Lawrence, sonority about death is now pretentious; and the poem insists upon the self-effacement and humility of holy dying, the weakness and ordinariness of persons as death in its mystery envelops them.

The soul travels over an unknown sea in sections VII and VIII, drawn into an increasing density of oblivion that is reminiscent of "Bavarian Gentians." But the flood of death subsides at the first thread of dawn over the sea, in sections IX and X. The little ship returns, and the soul re-enters the body that "like a worn sea-shell/emerges strange and lovely." That journey to the edge of eternity, which Lawrence felt that he experienced every night in solitude, darkness and sleep, renews his heart with peace. The morning—that is only "a flush of yellow" and "a flush of rose"—both cruelly and gently gives him another day to prepare for his farthest voyage.

"The Ship of Death" comes to a conclusion that suggests parallels with the concluding emotion and final situation in nearly all his major writings. From *The White Peacock* to his very last works, Lawrence's best art considers the plight of human individuality in an immensely powerful, obscure universe. He wrote about the unconscious determination of man's relationships within a family, in marriage, in society and with the natural world. In his intuitive, highly symbolic art he projected the tragic drama of his inner life onto the world around him, and he progressively uncovered the deep motivations of his character in his sympathies with natural life. Because America seemed to promise eventual freedom from internal as well as external oppression, the Southwest became symbolically encoded with the basic conflicts and purposes of his soul. When he could no longer sustain the crucial personal revelation during his American experience, his orientation toward a future era of liberated sensual sympathies among all independent beings changed into the detached narcissism of his later fiction. But even in dying away from the world he continued to uphold a sense of his personal identity existing within inexhaustible and holy life. In his death poems and his essay on the Etruscan tombs—as more or less consciously in all his works—he acknowledges that beyond the griefs of manhood or modernity the isolation of the soul is the one dreadful obstruction in the way of vivid, perfect experience.

Notes

CHAPTER I

1. *Literary Essays of Ezra Pound*, New Directions, 1954, p. 9.
2. *The Letters of Ezra Pound, 1907–1941*, Harcourt Brace, 1950, p. 17.
3. *Literary Essays*, pp. 387–88.
4. *Form and Value in Modern Poetry*, Doubleday Anchor Books, 1957, p. 256.
5. Blackmur's criticism of Lawrence is answered by David Gordon, *D. H. Lawrence as a Literary Critic*, Yale University Press, 1966.

CHAPTER 2

1. Harry T. Moore, after examining the *Paul Morel* manuscript that comprises "parts of two earlier versions," concludes that: "The *Paul Morel* fragments are too sketchy to warrant much critical comment, except it may be said that the scenes—often the seeds for later development in the final version of the novel— rarely come to life. They are not organically arranged, and the people lack the vitality of those in *Sons and Lovers*. Apparently it was not until after Lawrence had met Frieda Weekeley-Richthofen, and went away to live with her in Germany and Italy, that he could see his past experience in perspective and at last make *Sons and Lovers* the coherent—and great—novel which Duckworth published in 1913." *D. H. Lawrence and "Sons and Lovers": Sources and Criticism*, edited by E. W. Tedlock, Jr., New York University Press, 1965, pp. 63–65.

Keith Sagar also attributes great importance to Frieda's influence over the composition of *Sons and Lovers* in his study of *The Art of D. H. Lawrence*, Cambridge University Press, 1966, p. 35.

2. Many writers follow John Middleton Murry's "diagnosis" of Lawrence's relationship with Frieda in his two books, *Son of Woman*, Jonathan Cape, 1931; and *Reminiscences of D. H. Lawrence*, Jonathan Cape, 1933.

3. Anthony West offers an interesting comparison of the two women in *D. H. Lawrence*, Barker, 1950, pp. 23–26. West maintains that "they were as utterly different in their habits of mind as in their physique."

4. Frieda Lawrence, *The Memoirs and Correspondence*, edited by E. W. Tedlock, Jr., Heinemann, 1961, pp. 185–86.

5. *"Not I, But The Wind . . . ,"* Viking Press, 1934, p. 56.

6. E. W. Tedlock, Jr., *D. H. Lawrence, Artist and Rebel*, University of New Mexico Press, 1963, p. 42.

7. For a demonstration of the novel's vagueness about crucial events, see Sagar, p. 11.

8. Sagar, wishing to correct a prevalent distortion of Mrs. Morel as a soul-devouring harridan, declares that "there is a destructive element in her relations with husband and sons; but the overriding impression is of a normality and strength of character which serves as a standard against which other women in the novel are judged, and found wanting." See "The Bases of the Normal," in *The Art of D. H. Lawrence*, pp. 19–35. Sagar's redemption of Mrs. Morel disregards the grotesque and prominent abnormalities of her relations with Paul, which are the thematic point of the novel.

9. I am indebted to Daniel Weiss's psychoanalytic study of *Sons and Lovers* for my basic perspective on the novel. For his excellent analysis of subconscious determination in the creative process, see *Oedipus in Nottingham: D. H. Lawrence*, University of Washington Press, 1962.

10. H. M. Daleski makes a close stylistic comparison of the two episodes in *The Forked Flame: A Study of D. H. Lawrence*, Northwestern University Press, 1965, pp. 57–59. Daleski might have further pointed out the prominently recurring fire imagery of the hearth in Gertrude's sick-room, and Paul's view of his dying mother "wasted to a fragment of ash," details which recapitulate young Paul's ritual of burning the doll. Also, the psychological significance of the earlier episode is supported by the name that

Lawrence gave the doll, for "Missis Arabella" condenses Gertrude's double role which so distressingly confuses Paul. The doll faintly bears the names of the virginal Gertrude Coppard and the wife Gertrude Morel.

11. George Ford draws attention to Gertrude Morel as one of the figures of Persephone in Lawrence's repeated use of that motif in his fictions about "the dark man and fair woman." *Double Measure: A Study of the Novels and Stories of D. H. Lawrence*, Holt, Rinehart & Winston, 1965.

Mark Spilka's analysis of the prominent flower symbolism throughout *Sons and Lovers* supports the relevance of the Persephone myth. See *The Love Ethic of D. H. Lawrence*, Indiana University Press, 1955, pp. 39–59.

CHAPTER 3

1. For a brief, sensitive memoir of Lawrence that bears on his relations with many of the Bloomsbury intellectuals during this period, see J. M. Keynes, *Two Memoirs*, A. M. Kelley, 1949.

2. For the national background of Lawrence's economic proposals, see Charles Loch Mowat, *Britain Between the Wars, 1918–1940*, The University of Chicago Press, 1955; also Richard W. Lyman, *The First Labour Government, 1924*, Chapman and Hall, 1958.

3. *The Rise of the Novel: Studies in Defoe, Richardson and Fielding*, The University of California Press, 1957.

4. Roger Sale demonstrates Lawrence's generalizing devices in another episode of *The Rainbow* in "The Narrative Technique of *The Rainbow*," *Modern Fiction Studies*, V (Spring 1959), 30–32.

5. For a general account of the Futurists, see Rose Trillo Clough, *Futurism, The Story of a Modern Art Movement*, Philosophical Library, 1961.

6. F. R. Leavis takes a contrary view about "that confident note of prophetic hope in the final paragraph—a note wholly unprepared and unsupported, defying the preceding pages." *D. H. Lawrence: Novelist*, Knopf, 1956, p. 170.

7. A fuller account of the suppression action and the probable political overtones in it appears in Harry T. Moore, *The Intelligent Heart: The Story of D. H. Lawrence*, Farrar, Strauss, and Young, 1954, pp. 199–203. Lawrence's letters are filled with references to the suppression from November 6 to December 4, 1915.

8. The relevant excerpts from Pound's letter to Iris Barry indicate

the industry's fear of the public mood, and the letter includes an amusing reference to Yeats:

> If by any chance you intended to get my new volume of poems *Lustra* when it comes out, then do for God's sake order your copy at once and UNABRIDGED.
> The idiot Mathews has got the whole volume set up in type, and has now got a panic and marked 25 poems for deletion. Most of them have already been printed in magazines without causing any scandal whatever, and some of them are among the best in the book. . . .
> The scrape is both serious and ludicrous. Some of the poems will have to go, but in other cases the objections are too stupid for words. It is part printer and part Mathews.
>
> . . . .
>
> The printers have gone quite mad since the Lawrence fuss. Joyce's new novel has gone to America (AMERICA!) to be printed by an enthusiastic publisher. Something has got to be done or we'll all of us be suppressed, a la counter-reformation, dead and done for.
> P.S. Elkin Mathews——called in Yeats to mediate and Yeats quoted Donne at him for his soul's good. I don't know what will come of it.
>
> *The Letters of Ezra Pound*, pp. 80–81.

9. "The final version of *Women in Love* was completed in 1916 while the Lawrences were living in Cornwall; Catherine Carswell records her reactions after reading a typescript in November of that year. Mrs. Carswell says that almost every publisher in London refused the manuscript. Methuen cancelled their contract with Lawrence after reading it, and Duckworth also refused to accept the novel for publication. Lawrence anticipated the trouble he would have and wrote to Lady Cynthia Asquith asking her to suggest a patron who would accept a 'serious dedication' and thus afford the book protection which could prevent the sort of trouble *The Rainbow* experienced. These efforts were in vain, however, for publication had to wait for almost five years, and then it was privately printed in New York." Warren Roberts, *A Bibliography of D. H. Lawrence*, Rupert Hart-Davis, 1963, p. 45.

10. By M[aurice] M[agnus], London, 1924. The essay is reprinted in *Phoenix Two*.

11. "The structural principle of *Women in Love* is locative; that is to say, there is a calculated movement from one place to another, each place being a representative unit in the social organism and serving as the focus of a local significance. The places are related to one another not merely through a juxtaposition which yields a comprehensive view of the social scene as a whole, but—so to speak—through their common location on volcanic soil. There are five such foci in the book: Beldover . . . Shortlands . . . Breadalby . . . the Cafe Pompadour . . . the Tyrolese hostel. . . . We are required, in each place, to register the tell-tale tremors which herald an inevitable cataclysm." *The Forked Flame: A Study of D. H. Lawrence*, Northwestern University Press, 1965, p. 128.

12. "D. H. Lawrence and *Women in Love*," in *Critical Essays*, Routledge and Kegan Paul, 1966, pp. 264–84.

13. In a letter to Murry, dated 6 August 1953, Frieda comments on the past friendship between the two men: "There was a real bond between you and L. If he had lived longer and had been older, you would have been real friends, he wanted so desperately for you to understand him. I think the homosexuality in him was a short phase out of misery—I fought him and won—and that he wanted a deeper thing from you. I am aware so much as I am old, of the elements in us, that we consist of. Do you know what I mean?" *Memoirs and Correspondence*, p. 328.

CHAPTER 4

1. The eight essays of version 1 that were printed in the *English Review* and the Whitman essay of version 2 that was printed in *The Nation and The Athenaeum*, 1921, are reprinted in *The Symbolic Meaning, The Uncollected Versions of "Studies in Classic American Literature*," edited by Armin Arnold, Centaur Press, 1962. Arnold includes three previously unpublished portions from version 2, completing the publication of all extant chapters written before Lawrence's final revision for his *Studies in Classic American Literature*, Seltzer, 1923.

An earlier book by Arnold, *D. H. Lawrence and America*, Philosophical Library, 1959, draws attention to Lawrence's increasing interest in the United States and his involvement with Americans. The major part of the book points out differences between the first and third versions of the essays on American writers, and includes a survey of critical opinions about the value of *Classic American Literature*.

2. In a memoir of their youthful love, Jessie Chambers discusses the reading that they shared. She mentions: "He read and liked Emerson's *Essays* and became wildly enthusiastic over Thoreau's *Walden*, especially the essay on 'The Ponds.'" E. T. [Jessie Chambers], *D. H. Lawrence, A Personal Record*, Jonathan Cape, 1935, p. 101.

3. Printed in the issue of December 15, 1920, the article is collected in *Phoenix*, pp. 87–91.

4. "Certain Americans and an Englishman," *New York Times Magazine*, December 24, 1922, p. 9.

5. Relevant letters and biographical discussion appear in *The Intelligent Heart*, pp. 251–52; and in S. Foster Damon, *Amy Lowell*, Houghton Mifflin, 1935, pp. 497–99 and pp. 513–14.

CHAPTER 5

1. The James Tait Black Prize of Edinburgh University, 1921.

2. I have appropriated a term from Wilhelm Reich's writings and used it to describe Lawrence's studies of psychology partly to suggest the parallels between Reich's and Lawrence's views of the "biopsychic structure" of man. Reich did most of his clinical work and writing in Germany during the 1920's and early 1930's.

3. Allen Guttmann discusses Lawrence's fascist ideas in "D. H. Lawrence: The Politics of Irrationality," *Wisconsin Studies in Contemporary Literature*, V (Summer 1964), 151–63. John Harrison discusses the attraction of fascist ideas for several British and American writers, including a chapter on Lawrence, in *The Reactionaries*, Schocken, 1966.

4. Lawrence wrote *Sea and Sardinia* swiftly in the spring of 1921. By June of the same year he completed *Aaron's Rod*, which had been in progress from 1918.

   Page numbers in the text refer to the Compass Books edition, New York, 1963.

5. M[aurice] M[agnus], London, 1924. Murry recollects that "in the winter of 1923 Lawrence told me he thought that introduction [to the *Memoirs*] was the best thing he had ever written. . . . But I think the importance he attached to it was due less to the mastery of his medium which it showed than to the fact that it contained the record of a crucial experience in Lawrence's life." *Son of Woman*, p. 152.

Edward Nehls also gives this Introduction central importance in Lawrence's life, in "D. H. Lawrence: The Spirit of Place," *The Achievement of D. H. Lawrence*, edited by Frederick J. Hoffman and Harry T. Moore, University of Oklahoma Press, 1953, pp. 268–90. The Introduction has been collected in *Phoenix II*.

6. In her book *Lorenzo in Taos*, Knopf, 1932, Mabel Dodge Luhan says: "It was after reading *Sea and Sardinia* that I wrote to him to come to Taos." From Lawrence's answer to her first letter it is clear that she had read enough of the work to make reference to "the q–b." But since her invitation arrived in Sicily on November 5th and the book was not published until December 12th, it is likely that she first read Lawrence in the few chapters that were printed as magazine pieces in the *Dial* for October and November 1921.

7. Earl and Achsah Brewster, *D. H. Lawrence, Reminiscences and Correspondence*, Secker, 1934.

8. *D. H. Lawrence and America*, p. 41.

9. See Luhan; also Knud Merrild, *A Poet and Two Painters*, Routledge, 1938; and Witter Bynner, *Journey With Genius*, John Day, 1951.

10. "Au Revoir, U. S. A.," *Phoenix*, pp. 104–6.

11. Merrild, p. 348.

12. These events are freely recollected in correspondence between Frieda and Murry from 1946 to 1955, collected in *Frieda Lawrence, the Memoirs and Correspondence*. Murry's biographer discusses the triangle of love and includes relevant passages from Murry's journal, in F. A. Lea, *The Life of John Middleton Murry*, Oxford University Press, 1960, pp. 117–20.

13. The Café Royal was the scene of an earlier humiliation in Lawrence's life, when his newly published *Amores* was maliciously burlesqued by a group of his acquaintances. Katherine Mansfield rescued the book from the hands of the reader and fled with it out of the café, an incident that Lawrence commemorated fictionally by Gudrun's similar action in the Café Pompadour in *Women in Love*. In the novel the Pompadour is made to represent Hell.

14. Relevant conflicting accounts by Murry and Mrs. Carswell are reprinted in Edward Nehls, *D. H. Lawrence, A Composite Biography*, University of Wisconsin Press, 1958, Vol. II, pp. 295–303.

15. "Smile," "The Border Line," "Jimmy and the Desperate Woman," and "The Last Laugh" are all impelled by animosity toward Murry.

CHAPTER 6

1. Dorothy Brett was an art student and an acquaintance of the late Katherine Mansfield when she met Lawrence on his visit to London and answered his call for followers to New Mexico. She wrote about her life at Kiowa in *Lawrence and Brett*, Lippincott, 1933.

2. This chapter develops, but differs in judgment and method, from Graham Hough's suggestive comments in *The Dark Sun: A Study of D. H. Lawrence*, Macmillan, 1957, pp. 117–48. The claims made in those pages spurred my attention to the entire subject of America's importance to Lawrence. Hough states that Lawrence in *The Plumed Serpent* "is trying to deal with what was perhaps the central revelation of his life." According to him, Lawrence failed personally to achieve an integration of character in the "almost maniacal" psychological adventure that he undertook without any "external guidance and support." In America, Lawrence "had his glimpse into the abyss, hesitated on the brink, and in the end turned back appalled. But the mere glimpse was enough to effect a permanent alteration." In spite of his intuition to the crisis of Lawrence's career, Hough's criticism and insight remain vague and uninformative.

3. The principal critical viewpoints are established by F. R. Leavis, who treats the tale as a major "dramatic poem," in *D. H. Lawrence: Novelist*, Knopf, 1956; and by Hough, who objects to the tale's implausibilities, in *The Dark Sun*.

4. Kingsley Widmer, *The Art of Perversity: D. H. Lawrence's Shorter Fictions*, University of Washington Press, 1962, p. 33.

5. For a discussion of the Pan theme in Lawrence's work, see Patricia Merivale, "D. H. Lawrence and the Modern Pan Myth," *Texas Studies in Literature and Language*, VI (1964), 297–305.

6. The essays were printed separately as magazine articles in 1924, and later Lawrence included them in his third travel book, *Mornings in Mexico*, Secker, 1927. In this discussion, page references to the essays cite the first American edition, Knopf, 1927.

For an article on the book of travel sketches as a unified work, see Thomas Whitaker, "Lawrence's Western Path: 'Mornings in Mexico,'" *Criticism*, III (1961), 219–36.

7. Dexter Martin in an article "D. H. Lawrence and Pueblo Religion: An Inquiry into Accuracy," comes to the conclusion that Lawrence's minor inaccuracies arise mainly from his desire to present persuasively what *he* could believe if he were an Indian. *Arizona Quarterly*, IX (1953), 219–34.

CHAPTER 7

1. The symbolism and other aspects of the novel are discussed in L. D. Clark, *Dark Night of the Body: D. H. Lawrence's "The Plumed Serpent,"* University of Texas Press, 1964.
2. Brewster, *Reminiscences and Correspondence*, p. 288.

CHAPTER 8

1. *Lady Chatterley's Lover* was first published in Florence in 1928. It was not allowed to be published or distributed in the United States until the Grove Press edition of 1959, or in England until the Penguin edition of 1960. Both publishing events were followed by highly publicized court trials of charges that the book was obscene.

   A Propos of "Lady Chatterley's Lover" was first written as an introductory essay for the Paris popular edition of the novel in 1929. The essay was greatly expanded and given its present title later in the year, and published separately as a pamphlet.
2. Comparisons of the three versions appear in Tedlock's *Descriptive Bibliography*, pp. 279–316, and in Mark Schorer's Introduction to the Grove Press edition of the novel, pp. xxvii–xxxvi.
3. *The Quest for Love*, University of Alabama Press, 1965, pp. 192–333.
4. Compass Books, 1966, pp. 199–200. *Apocalypse* was first published posthumously in 1931.
5. *Etruscan Places* was published posthumously in 1932 from travel sketches that Lawrence had not revised entirely to his satisfaction. Page citations refer to the Compass edition, 1963.
6. "D. H. Lawrence and the Etruscans," *Essays by Diverse Hands*, XXXI (1962), 61–78.

Index

229